THE TOSHIBA BOOK OF
Microwave Cookery
ANNEMARIE ROSIER

A WOODHEAD-FAULKNER PUBLICATION

Woodhead-Faulkner Ltd
8 Market Passage
Cambridge CB2 3PF

First published 1978
Reprinted with revisions 1980

© Toshiba (UK) Limited 1978, 1980

ISBN 0 85941 074 9

Designed by Ken Vail

Printed in Great Britain by
Lowe & Brydone Printers Ltd, Thetford, Norfolk

Foreword

by Sally Broad
General Manager, Toshiba Microwave Ovens

I have known Annemarie Rosier since I bought my first microwave oven six years ago and acknowledge her without hesitation as one of the most experienced microwave home economists.

I am delighted that she agreed to write *The Toshiba Book of Microwave Cookery* and feel sure that you, the reader, will get much enjoyment from it.

Sally Broad

Author's Preface

When I was first at my senior school, I went to visit a food exhibition and there I saw what to me was a magic box. Food put in cold came out hot in seconds – the demonstrator needed no oven gloves even when she cooked a steamed sponge pudding in a minute. Pure magic. From that moment my dreams of becoming a great singer or train driver were finished. I wanted to work with the magic box, and now, after ten years of cooking with the microwave oven, I still feel as enthusiastic.

The microwave oven has changed in design and technology since I first saw it, but still remains a superb defroster of frozen foods, cooker of raw foods, and fast heater of precooked items. If you enjoy cooking, this oven, with its speed and its ability to retain the flavour and colour of food, will increase your enjoyment and, for those who dislike cooking, the labour-saving benefits of microwave will be an absolute boon.

This book has been divided into three parts. The first part deals with how the oven works and how to use it to its full advantage. The second part contains recipes and timings on heating and defrosting with the oven. All of the timings have been done on a 620-watt oven but are easily convertible for other power ovens. The third part deals with the variable power control oven, but some of the recipes in that section can be done in standard ovens.

Before starting to cook with your oven, do read the first part of the book. The transition from conventional cooking to microwave is simple once the basic principles have been noted. Then turn to the recipes; many will be old favourites, but see how short the cooking time is, and taste the results – good fresh hot food.

Happy microwave cooking!   A. R.

Contents

**Part Three: Variable Power
Control Microwave**

PART ONE
Introducing the Microwave Oven

Note: All recipes in this book serve four people unless otherwise stated.

Installation, Operation and Cleaning of the Oven

WHERE TO PUT THE MICROWAVE OVEN

Place the oven on a working surface or strong shelf which is at a convenient height, preferably near to a 13-amp socket. As the oven creates very few smells, steam or grease in the room, there is no need for the oven to be near an extraction unit. If you would like the oven built into your kitchen, ask your microwave distributor, who will be able to advise you on this. Sometimes in a kitchen there is a shortage of space, so remember that the oven can be placed on a trolley and wheeled wherever it is required, even into the garden for summer meals.

Remove all the packaging from inside the oven but make sure you do not throw away the guarantee card – in fact fill it in right away and send it off.

Plug the oven into a 13-amp socket and you are ready to cook.

OPERATING THE OVEN

Never operate the oven without food or liquid inside. Microwave ovens all differ in some small details and the instructions accompanying any one model should be carefully studied.

Having connected the oven to a 13-amp socket, you should check its operation by placing a cup of water inside. Set timer to 1 minute and press 'Cook' button. The oven will now be operating. At the end of the cooking period the timer will have moved back to the zero position and a bell will sound. The oven will then no longer be sending energy into the cavity.

Open the oven door and remove the water, which should be warm. The oven cannot be operated with the oven door open. Some microwave ovens are operated by setting the timer and will switch off completely when the cooking cycle ends. There is no need to wait for the oven to 'warm up'. It is instantly ready to use.

CLEANING THE OVEN

One of the many joys of a microwave oven is how clean

the cavity stays. Because the food is generally covered in the oven there is little splashing, and as there is no direct heat and the oven walls stay cool, the marks that occur are not baked on.

To clean the oven, wipe it out with a damp cloth after every meal. Do not use steel wool on the surface or any harsh cleaners as they may scratch the oven surface and distort the heat pattern. Stubborn marks can be removed with a mild cleanser or by boiling water in the oven where the steam will loosen them, making the oven easy to wipe clean. The tray can be washed in the kitchen sink in warm soapy water, dried and returned to the oven.

Some microwave ovens have a filter at the base, which cleans the air passed through the oven to cool the electrical components. This filter should be washed in warm soapy water, dried and replaced once a month. The outside casing of the oven can be wiped over with a damp cloth and polished lightly with a spray polish.

For the oven to operate at peak efficiency the filter and cavity must be clean.

Microwave – What it is and how it works

The microwave oven is very different from a conventional cooker in both appearance and operation. In size and design it seems more like a television set; the controls are similar, too, as are some of the components used inside. In your gas or conventional electric oven, the air is heated, which cooks the outer surfaces of the food; the heat is then passed slowly into the centre of the food by conduction from molecule to molecule. By the time the centre is cooked, the outer surfaces have browned. The hot air in the oven also heats the container that holds the food and the walls of the oven. In a microwave oven the food is heated quickly outside and in. With quick-cooking items this means that the oven will be too fast to brown the outside of the food.

The food is cooked by electromagnetic waves which come into the cooking cavity at a very fast rate (2,450 million times per second). As with all waves they are reflected off the sides of the metal cavity and form a criss-cross pattern in the oven. The food absorbs the waves from all directions. These waves cause the moisture molecules in the food to vibrate, giving friction, which is heat. If you rub your hands together you are creating friction and you will feel heat; this is just what happens inside the food in the oven.

In the microwave oven, unlike your conventional cooker, only the food will be heated. The waves will pass straight through glass, china and paper, etc., without causing friction to the molecule structure. The main type of molecule to be affected by microwaves is water, and these materials contain none. As the sides of the oven are metal, which can only reflect the waves, no energy is wasted in heating anything but the food. This also means that the cooking containers and oven cavity are easy to clean.

In the diagram the main components of the microwave oven have been indicated.

1 *Lead from oven to plug.* This is plugged into a 13-amp socket, from which the power is drawn into the oven.

2 *Power pack.* This converts the voltage to that suitable to energise the magnetron.

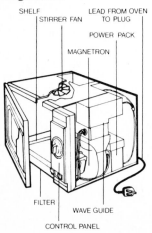

3 *Magnetron*. This is the heart of the oven; it converts the higher voltage to microwaves, which are very short waves similar to radio and television waves.

4 *Wave guide*. The waves are directed along the wave guide from the magnetron to the cavity.

5 *Stirrer fan*. This fan at the top of the cavity is made of several metal blades revolving slowly. These throw the waves into different directions in the cavity to give an even cooking pattern.

6 *Shelf*. The food in the oven is raised about an inch off the floor of the oven by a glass shelf to ensure absorption of the waves from all directions.

7 *Controls and door*. On the front of the oven are the controls and the door. The controls vary from oven to oven, but always include a clock which times the cooking process. The door is double-glazed for ease of cleaning with a wire mesh grill in-between.

8 *Filter*. Microwave ovens have air-cooling systems for the components. Air is pulled in at the base of the oven through a filter, directed around the main electrical workings and then taken out of the oven. The filter prevents dust entering the mechanism.

Note: All microwave ovens are fitted with an automatic cut-out which operates when the door is opened or timing ceased.

Getting to Know your Oven

The microwave oven is really many appliances combined into one unit. No other piece of kitchen equipment can do so many jobs so successfully. The oven can be used for the heating of cooked food – the roast joint left over from Sunday can be served hot on Monday without drying or toughening the meat or losing any flavour. If members of your family are eating later there is no need to cook a meal when they arrive or to keep food warm in a conventional oven; cook their portion with the rest and reheat as required.

Frozen food can be defrosted rapidly in the oven. No longer do you have to remember to remove food from the freezer the night before – decide what you would like to eat and defrost in minutes in the oven.

The microwave oven can also be used for the majority of your prime cooking, from joints of meat, vegetables and cakes to scrambled eggs. On the cooking side, it will not completely replace your conventional cooker as there are some things it will not do, such as baking a soufflé, setting meringues or boiling an egg in its shell, but the many uses of the oven make it a valuable appliance in any home.

All microwave operations are controlled by time – minutes and seconds. How long the food will take in the oven is controlled by various factors, and once these have been noted the timing becomes easy.

POWER OF THE OVEN

The timings for this book have been done on a 620-watt oven, but they are suitable for any power oven. The higher the power of the oven, the quicker the result. The lower the power, the slower the result. So in a lower-power oven more time has to be given, as a guideline approximately 20 seconds extra per minute, and on the higher-power ovens less time than stated will be used.

STARTING TEMPERATURE OF THE FOOD

The colder the food, the longer it will take to be heated or cooked by the waves. In conventional cooking, generally we are concerned with frozen food and room temperature food, but with the microwave oven there are three starting temperatures – frozen, refrigerated and room or ambient. A meat pie that is frozen will take perhaps 2 minutes to heat, from the refrigerator 1 minute, and if at ambient temperature 40 seconds.

AMOUNT OF FOOD PLACED IN THE OVEN

There is only a set amount of energy coming into the oven cavity. When one item of food is there all the energy is absorbed into it, so, when two or more items of food are placed into the cavity, the energy is shared between them; consequently this means the food will take longer. One plated meal to heat in the oven will take 2 minutes; two will take approximately 3½ minutes. Do not try to fill the microwave oven with food; it is quicker to heat or cook in small amounts.

SHAPE OF THE FOOD

The more even the shape of food, the better the result. It is better to bone and roll awkward-shaped joints of meat, *e.g.* leg of lamb, before cooking in the oven. If this is not possible a thin strip of foil can be placed around the narrower ends of meat and removed halfway through the cooking time, as this will even out the cooking result.

When cooking dishes with a heavy, thick consistency in a casserole, such as cheese and potato pie, you will find that it is quite difficult to achieve a cooked centre with this sort of dish. However, if you push a tumbler, base first, into the centre of the dish, in effect producing a hollow centre to the cheese and potato pie, you will have no problem cooking it. This is because the awkward centre will have been eliminated.

DENSITY OF THE FOOD

When the food has a light, open texture it will be quicker to heat than solid items; *e.g.* a sponge pudding is quicker to heat than a steak and kidney pudding. This is because the waves can penetrate into the food more easily.

STANDING TIME

Food when removed from the oven should be left to stand for a few minutes before serving. It will not get cold because it is still cooking. The friction that is created within the food continues working and producing heat. The longer the food is in the oven, the greater the continuation of cooking on removal.

COVERS

By covering food in the microwave oven, steam is trapped, enabling some food items to be cooked in the minimum amount of liquid, so ensuring no loss of flavour. This also helps contribute to even and slightly faster cooking. Covering a utensil will make it tend to become hot at the edges, so be careful when removing the container from the oven. Covering of the food prevents splashing in the oven. Do not cover any food item that needs to be kept fairly dry, *e.g.* pastry products or when cooking cakes.

The recipes in this book will show you how easily you can become familiar with all these points when using the microwave oven, so do not worry if they seem involved at the moment – remember, so did driving a car, feeding a husband or bathing a baby before you began to try.

Heating Food by Microwave

The microwave oven heats food without drying it or losing any of the colour or flavour. Cooking can be done in advance at any time, the food being left covered in the refrigerator and reheated as required. Left-overs are easily used the following day, either as part of a dish or as a meal on their own. Any canned food just requires the can being opened and the contents placed on a serving dish and heated in the oven. Members of the family can use the oven to heat their own snacks or meals if you are not there. Where there is a baby in the house, bottles can be prepared in advance and heated quickly and safely as required.

Timings for heating food are given in the relevant sections in Part Two, but these general guidelines should always be borne in mind:

1 Food left in a refrigerator should always be covered.
2 Where possible do not try to heat two dishes of different foods at the same time in the oven. As long as the food is kept covered it will remain warm for quite some time.
3 Any liquids or casserole-type dishes will require stirring during and after the heating period to ensure even heating.
4 Do not cover milk drinks during heating.
5 When heating large pies or flans, turn halfway through the cooking cycle.

PLATED MEALS
If more than one serving is required, two plates can be

stacked on top of each other in the oven by using a stacking ring. The top plate should be covered with another plate turned upside-down.

When plating a meal, all the food should be at the same cooked state and starting temperature. Place the food on the plate as evenly as possible. Keep the food within the well of the plate. Cover the plate during the heating cycle. Always place the thickest part of an item of food towards the edge of the plate. Gravy or meat juice should be poured over the meat before heating. Leave the meal to stand covered for a few seconds before serving.

One 12 oz plated meal in the oven will take approximately 2 minutes to reheat.

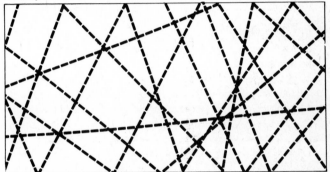

Microwaves bounce off walls of cavity and into food from all directions

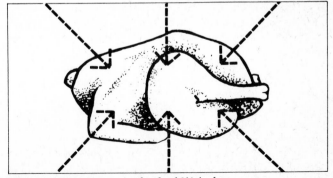

Microwaves penetrate to a depth of 1½ inches

15

Defrosting Food by Microwave

The freezer and microwave oven make ideal companions – how often have you forgotten to remove the lunch from the freezer and it's been cheese on toast again, or served, because you are in a hurry, a half-defrosted cake. With the microwave oven, food defrosts in minutes without any loss of flavour or problems with bacteria.

When food is frozen, ice crystals are formed inside the product; these have sharp edges and tend to reflect the microwaves. For this reason when defrosting by microwave the oven is used in a different way – the food is placed in the oven and then subjected to a burst of waves which ensures that the ice crystals are evenly broken down.

If your oven has a special defrost switch for this purpose, the waves are pulsed on and off automatically. Where there is no defrost switch, this process can be done manually by placing the food in the oven, giving it half the defrost time, letting the food rest for a few minutes and then heating it for a further period. With both methods the food must be left to rest before further cooking or reheating. Check that the food is completely defrosted by feel; if it needs longer, return to the oven for a short time and rest again.

Leave the food covered during the defrosting cycle except for all bakery products. Any item wrapped in foil should be turned into a covered dish.

Defrosting timings will be found in the cookery sections in Part Two with special reference notes to the products.

If using a *500-watt* oven without a defrost switch the following approximate timings will be useful:

Food	1st heat	Rest	2nd heat
1 standard loaf of bread	2 mins	4 mins	1 min
2 bread rolls	30 secs	1 min	30 secs
1 frozen pastry	15 secs	30 secs	10 secs
1 cream sponge cake	20 secs	3 mins	20 secs
Plated meal	3 mins	3 mins	1½ mins
1 lb frozen fruit	2 mins	3 mins	1 min

Food	1st heat	Rest	2nd heat
Boil-in-the-bag product	2 mins	3 mins	2 mins
Family-size cottage pie	4 mins	5 mins	2 mins
2 lamb chops	2 mins	1 min	½ min
1 steak	1 min	2 mins	½ min
1 lb fish	1½ mins	2 mins	1½ mins
Single portion of fish	1 min	2 mins	1 min
1 lb prawns	3 mins	2 mins	2 mins
1 lb chicken pieces	3 mins	5 mins	3 mins
Whole chicken per lb	3 mins	5 mins	3 mins
Joints of meat per lb	3 mins	3 mins	2 mins

It is advisable to turn all foods after the first heating stage.

Cooking by Microwave

The microwave oven as a prime cooker of food has many advantages over conventional cooking methods. The time-saving element can be as much as 75 per cent on some items, but speed advantages alone would be of no consequence if the end result suffered. Food cooked in a microwave oven will have better flavour and colour retention; also the vitamin and mineral content of the food will not be lost to the same degree as when cooking conventionally.

Part Two of the book gives details of specific points to note when cooking different foods in the oven but there are some points which relate to all foods.

PAST EXPERIENCE
Do not think of the microwave oven as a magic box and forget about the basic rules of cooking. Cooking is a science and the process of concocting and cooking a dish is done in a certain way and order for good reasons. With the microwave oven, the order of preparing a dish is not drastically altered, the ingredients only slightly, and the cooking is faster than you have been used to before. Take, for instance, a casserole – normally vegetables are sautéed, the meat sealed, then stock and seasoning added, and it is

the same when using the oven. If all the ingredients were thrown into a casserole at the same time, the end result would be uneven.

TURNING THE FOOD
Most foods during their cooking cycle will be either turned or stirred. This helps the food to cook evenly and quickly in the oven. The food is not affected by opening the oven door. When a recipe says turn the food it does not mean turn it over, but turn the dish around in the oven either a quarter, third or half turn depending on the number of turns the recipe states. As you become more familiar with the oven you may find you do not need to turn the food so often, but in the beginning use the book as a guide. If you have a turntable oven, you can ignore the 'turn' instruction in the recipe.

LIQUID
Very often the liquid content added to a dish may be more or less than that to which you are accustomed. This is because the microwave reacts mainly on the water molecules and, to ensure good cooking, adjustments have to be made.

SEASONING
Always adjust the seasoning to taste after cooking. Because of the speed of the oven, more seasoning than usual may be needed. Do not season vegetables until they are cooked.

TIMING
If you are not sure about a cooking time, set the oven for half of your estimation, check the contents and cook for longer, if required. It is better to undercook than overcook.

CHECKING
The cooking time that is necessary can normally be judged by texture, smell, colour, etc. If it needs longer cooking, return the dish to the oven but remember the food will carry on cooking for a time after removal from the microwave oven.

Utensils for the Microwave Oven

With the microwave oven the choice of cooking utensils is almost unlimited – because the microwaves only affect the water content of an item and very few kitchen or serving containers have water-based structures. Consequently, most non-metal containers can be used in the oven and will not be heated or damaged. In fact the waves will pass straight through them, only heating the food they hold. A certain amount of heat will of course be conducted by the food to the utensil.

Serving dishes can now be used for cooking and serving, helping to cut down the washing-up dramatically. Frozen foods can often be defrosted and heated in the plastic container in which they are purchased, or even in paper plates, serviettes and towels. There are no more burnt saucepans or awkward containers to clean when using the oven.

There is, however, one big NO – and that is to metal pots and pans in the oven. Metal reflects the waves in the oven and prevents any food from becoming heated. Over a period of time metal will also damage the oven, making dents to the cavity and ruining the heating pattern. So forget what it is like to scrub and scour pans – take a look around the kitchen and in the china and glass cupboard and meet your new cooking utensils.

CHINA

China tableware can be used throughout the day in the oven, from cooking the morning porridge in the cereal bowl to late at night when heating milk drinks in china mugs. Do not use the china if it has a gold or silver design on the plate, as 'arcing' – blue flashes of light – will occur and ruin the pattern. Any cups or plates stuck or mended with glue should also not be used as the glue may melt.

TOUGHENED GLASS AND CERAMICS

Most Pyrex and Pyrosil containers are ideal for the oven. As with the china, the same rule applies – those with metallic edges or patterns must not be used. Most of the recipes in this book have been cooked in one or other of these types of utensil.

PAPER
Paper plates, towels and napkins can be used for heating food on. Frozen food packaged in paper containers can be used for the defrosting cycle and reheating, but if the food is raw it is not advisable to cook in this type of container as the juices from the food will make the material too wet.

PLASTIC
Plastics that cannot be broken by tearing or crushing in the hand and that are recommended for use in a dishwasher are suitable for the microwave oven. For short-term heating in the oven, freezer, picnic and storage containers are ideal. Do not heat strongly coloured foods such as baked beans in them as the colour may stain the container. Foods with a high sugar or fat content should not be overheated when using plastics, as they may cause melting. Babies' bottles can safely be heated in the oven. Any plastics designed for use as 'boil-in-the-bag' containers are ideal; prick before use. Do not use standard plastic bags in the oven as they will melt on to the food.

Melamine and similar table utensils should not be used in the oven as they absorb microwaves.

GLASS
Do not use crystal glass in the oven as this contains a proportion of lead and may crack during heating; the same applies to thin-stemmed glasses. Otherwise all glass is suitable.

WOOD
Wood platters and steak plates may be used for short heating times in the oven. Avoid placing wooden items in the oven if parts have been joined with glue; this also applies to wooden-handled pastry brushes as the bristles are held in the handle with glue.

STRAW
Straw baskets can be used in the oven for short heating times.

POTTERY

Some pottery and earthenware dishes are not suitable for use in the oven because of the type of glaze used on them. A container that heats up while the food remains cool is not suitable for microwave oven usage.

COVERS

Many of the recipes in this book recommend covering the dish. For this you can use a casserole lid, a china plate, greaseproof paper or a cooking or cling film. *Do not use* aluminium foil. Take care when removing the cover from a cooking dish as steam will be trapped beneath the plate.

Note: The container you use in the oven will affect the timing of the food. This is because it alters the shape of whatever is being heated or cooked, so be prepared when first using the oven for timings to be slightly different from those stated.

Browning and Microwave

Browning of food occurs in a microwave oven when large items, *e.g.* a 3 lb joint of beef, is being cooked. This is due to the air around the meat becoming hot and the natural fats and sugars of the meat starting to caramelise, but with smaller items their time in the oven is too short for this to happen. Dishes requiring browning or crisping can be cooked in a browning dish or placed under the grill for a few minutes after cooking; this can also be done to joints of meat for a final touch.

Meat for casseroles can be coloured in a frying pan on top of the conventional cooker before being placed in the microwave oven. Sometimes all that is needed to complete a dish as regards colour and texture is a sprinkling of fried breadcrumbs, toasted almonds, crushed cereal or brown sugar. These can always be prepared in advance and stored in jars in the fridge or freezer and used as required.

For small cuts of fish and meat the Microwave Browning Dish can be used both for colouring and for cooking; see as an example the steak in illustration 1 in the colour section. The dish has been specially developed for the microwave oven and must not be used in a conventional one. It is made of a glass ceramic with a special coating on the base. When heated in a microwave oven it will absorb the microwaves and become very hot. Food that is placed on it browns on the contact side: by turning the food over, the other side is also coloured. The inside of the food is cooked by microwave. As food will absorb heat from the base of the browning dish it needs to be boosted in between cooking several items of food; just reheat the tray by itself for 1 minute or so and use again.

The browning dish cooking chart will give you an idea of timings; if you require a deeper colour, then heat the dish for longer than suggested. However, the manufacturers recommend not preheating for longer than 8 minutes.

Food	Additions	Preheat time (mins)	1st side (mins)	2nd side (mins)
Steak, 8 oz	Butter and season	4	2	1½
Hamburgers, 4 × 2 oz	Butter and season	3	2½	1½
Pork chops, 2 × 5 oz	Butter and season	4	2½	2
Lamb chops, 2 × 4 oz	Butter and season	3	2	1½
Egg	1 tbs oil after heating	3	1	Cover
Bacon, 2 rashers		3	1	1¼
Fish fingers, 4 frozen	2 tbs oil after heating	4	2	2
Chicken pieces, 2 × 4 oz	Flour chicken 2 tbs oil after heating	3½	2½	2½
Cheese dreams	1 tbs oil after heating	3	1½	1

It is also possible to use the browning dish for cooking a complete recipe. The following two recipes are an illustration of the variety of ways the browning dish can be used.

Paprika Liver

½ oz butter
salt and pepper
12 oz lamb's liver, well dried
1 small carton soured cream
1 level teaspoon paprika

Heat the browning dish in the oven for 4 minutes. Place the butter and seasoning into the dish; heat for a further 30 seconds. Press the liver firmly on to the surface of the dish, turn over and repeat. This will seal the liver on both sides. Cook the liver in the dish for 1¾ minutes; turn the liver over and cook for a further 1¾ minutes. Remove the liver from the dish and stand it to one side. Add the soured cream and paprika to the dish, mix well and cook for 2 minutes. Pour the sauce over the liver and serve.

Browning Dish Pizza

1 packet white bread mix
1 small can tomatoes
2 oz cooked ham
oil
oregano
grated cheese
salt and pepper

Make up the bread mix according to the directions on the packet. When the mix has proved, cut in half and roll out each piece to the size of the base of the browning dish. Heat the dish in the oven for 6 minutes. Grease well with the oil. Press in half the dough and cover with the tomatoes, seasoning and oregano. Cook for 2 minutes, sprinkle on the chopped ham and grated cheese. Cook for a further 5 minutes, remove from dish and serve.

PART TWO
Recipes and Timings

Menu Planning

Every item cooked in the microwave oven has a prepara-
tion time, a cooking time and a standing time. Because of
the short cooking times and the fact that microwave-
cooked food retains its heat for a long period, it is a simple
process to cook a complete meal in the oven. If any item of
food should be slightly cool when it comes to be served,
the dish can always be placed in the oven to boost the
temperature. Use the oven when you first get it to cook
just part of a meal and then progress to cooking a full
meal.

HINTS FOR SUCCESSFUL MEAL COOKERY
1   Defrost food first, except for vegetables.
2   Sweets to be served cold should be cooked in advance.
3   Soups, joints or casseroles should be cooked before
any vegetables.
4   The oven can be stopped at any time, the dish that is
cooking being removed, another placed in the oven, and
the original returned at a later time without ill effects on
the food.

MENU 1

	Cooking time
Tomato soup	19 mins
(see page 29)	
Crispy cod	9 mins
(see page 47)	
Mashed potato	10 mins
Peas	5 mins
Stuffed peaches	6 mins
(see page 62)	

Cook the tomato soup and divide into individual soup
bowls; the soup can then be reheated as required. Cook
the potatoes, season and mash. Leave in a covered serving
dish. Cook the bacon topping for the fish. Cook the fish
and add topping. Cover. Heat the soup. While the soup is
being eaten, the peas can be cooking. The peaches can be
cooking in the oven while the main course is being eaten.

	Cooking time
Hot grapefruit	5 mins
Roast pork, 3 lb	36 mins
Gravy	6 mins
Bavarian red cabbage	31 mins
(see page 56)	
Potatoes	10 mins
Pineapple upside-down pudding	8 mins
(see page 68)	

Cook the Bavarian cabbage and leave to one side. Cook the pork and cover. Cook the gravy. Cook the potatoes; place under the grill with the pork to colour and crispen. Heat the grapefruit and serve. Heat the cabbage while eating. Heat the gravy while changing plates, etc. The pineapple upside-down pudding will cook while the main course is being eaten.

When serving a large number of people at one meal, it is better to cook the vegetables in advance and heat when required, after removing the meat from the oven. Sauces should also be made in advance for large numbers and reheated. Before starting to cook a meal it is a good idea to write down a quick time plan for the dishes and their order of cooking. After a little practice, meal planning with the oven is simple, so don't be put off.

Soups

On a cold winter's day there is nothing so warming or satisfying as a bowl of home-made soup, and in the summer one of the nicest ways to begin a meal is with a delicate chilled soup. The microwave oven produces soups so quickly that it is almost quicker to make them than to open a can or packet.

HINTS FOR SUCCESSFUL SOUPS

1 Basic stocks for soups can be made in the microwave oven by combining the required ingredients in a large casserole dish and cooking for 30 minutes. Leave to stand for 30 minutes before using.

2 Use covers for the soups only when the recipe states so.

3 Milk-based soups should be cooked in containers large enough to allow for expansion of the liquid during boiling.

4 Stir several times during the cooking of the soup, to ensure evenness of heat and a smooth end result.

5 When preparing your own recipes in the microwave oven, use slightly less fat for sautéing vegetables. Add a little more liquid than normal.

6 When adding egg or cream to a soup, be careful not to overheat.

DEFROSTING SOUPS BY MICROWAVE

When freezing soups to be reheated in the microwave oven, do not add the egg or cream. This can be added after the defrosting cycle. A pint of frozen thick soup will take about 10 minutes to defrost, thin soup about 8 minutes. Stir the soup several times during defrosting.

REHEATING SOUPS BY MICROWAVE

Stir the soup during the heating cycle. For best results heat in a straight-sided container. One pint of soup will take approximately 6 to 8 minutes to reheat, a single portion 1½ minutes. Always stir before serving.

Canned Soups

Canned soups should be removed from the tin and stirred well before heating.

Dehydrated Soups

These soups should be mixed with hot water before placing into the oven. Heat for 4 to 6 minutes and allow to stand for 10 minutes. Heat again and stir before serving.

Tomato Soup

See illustration 2 in colour section

1 lb tomatoes, sliced
1 tablespoon instant potato mix
2 rashers streaky bacon
1 small onion, chopped
¼ pint milk
¼ pint water
1 teaspoon salt
1 teaspoon sugar
1 teaspoon paprika pepper
½ teaspoon celery salt
½ oz margarine
pinch of nutmeg

Melt margarine in the oven for 1 minute. Add the bacon and onion; sauté for 4 minutes. Add the sliced tomatoes, seasoning and potato powder. Mix well. Pour the water over the tomatoes, cover and return to the oven for 10 minutes. Liquidise or purée the soup, add the milk and return to the oven for 4 minutes.

Cream of Corn Soup

See illustration 2 in colour section

¼ pint water
8 oz frozen sweetcorn
1 oz margarine
2 level tablespoons flour
1 tablespoon chopped onion
pepper and salt
1 pint milk
3 rashers of bacon

Cook the bacon on absorbent paper in the microwave until crisp, approximately 3½ minutes. Remove from the oven and cool. Cook the corn in ¼ pint of water for 6 minutes. Put to one side. Melt the fat for 1 minute, add the onion and cook for 2 minutes. Remove from oven, add the flour, mix well and cook for 1 minute. Heat the milk for 3 minutes and slowly pour on to the flour, stirring well. Mix the corn and water into the milk. Place in the oven and cook for 9 minutes. Stir soup once during this cycle. On removal from the oven, season to taste and garnish with the crumbled bacon.

Lettuce Soup

See illustration 2 in colour section

8 oz lettuce leaves
salt
1 small onion, finely chopped
½ oz butter
¾ pint chicken stock
½ teaspoon caster sugar
pinch of nutmeg
croûtons

Place the lettuce in a covered container with 2 tablespoons of water. Heat in the oven for 2 minutes. Drain and rinse the lettuce under a cold tap. Shred the leaves finely. Melt butter in the oven for 45 seconds, add the onion and sauté for 2½ minutes. Add the lettuce, stock and seasoning and cook in the oven for 12 minutes. Stir once during this cycle. Remove the soup from the oven and purée or liquidise. Pour the milk into the soup, check the seasoning and return to the oven for 4 minutes. Just before serving, stir and garnish with croûtons.

Onion Soup

2 large onions, peeled and sliced
1½ oz butter
2 pints beef stock
salt
½ teaspoon paprika
2 teaspoons Worcester sauce

Melt the butter in a large dish for 1 minute. Add the onions, toss well in the butter and cook for 12 minutes. Remove the onions from the oven, stir and stand to one side covered. Heat the stock in the oven for 7 minutes. Add the onions and the other ingredients. Cook uncovered in the oven for 10 minutes. Serve with grated cheese and croûtons.

TWO QUICK CANNED SOUPS

Celery and Mushroom Soup

1 × 10 fl oz can cream of mushroom soup
1 × 10 fl oz can cream of celery soup
2 fl oz water
small carton of soured cream
chopped chives

Mix the soups and water well together. Heat in the oven for 8 minutes. Stir well. Garnish with sour cream and chives just before serving.

Chicken and Almond Soup for Two

1 × 10 fl oz can cream of chicken soup
½ oz butter
½ oz flaked almonds
1 dessertspoon chopped parsley

Melt the butter in the oven for 1 minute. Toss the parsley and almonds in the butter and heat for 6 to 7 minutes. Stir once during this cycle. The parsley should be crisp and the almonds golden brown. Open can of chicken soup and divide contents between two soup bowls. Heat for 3½ minutes in the oven. Stir and garnish with parsley and almonds just before serving.

Sauces

Sauces can be used in so many different ways, to add colour, flavour and texture to a dish, to bind ingredients together or to make a meal go further, but so often they seem a chore to make. With the microwave oven, sauces are easy to manage. They can be made in advance, being frozen or refrigerated and then heated as required, or they can be made during the cooking of a meal. You will find yourself happily adding that final gastronomic touch to the family's meal.

HINTS FOR SUCCESSFUL SAUCES

1   Good sauces need a lot of stirring to give them a smooth texture and a lovely shine, so don't be afraid to open the oven door and stir. The sauce will only be improved by so doing.
2   Try where possible to cook the sauce in the serving container as it saves on the washing-up.
3   Always cook milk-based sauces in a large container, as they tend to rise more rapidly when boiling than stock sauces.
4   Use a straight-sided container for cooking in where possible.
5   Do not cover the sauce during the cooking period unless the recipe states so.
6   Timings may vary slightly depending on the container used and the starting temperature of the ingredients.
7   If you require the sauce of a thicker consistency, cook it in the oven for a few seconds more than the time suggested.
8   Use the recipes in this section as a guideline for timings for your own favourite sauces.

DEFROSTING SAUCES BY MICROWAVE

Sauces are quicker to defrost if frozen in ice-cube trays. Add a small amount of liquor to the cubes, place in a covered container in the oven and heat for 3 minutes. Stir well and return to the oven until complete defrosting has finished.

When freezing the sauces in half-pint or pint containers, they will need between 10 and 15 minutes on defrost. Stir well to help distribute the heat during this time.

Sauces with sugar, *e.g.* apple sauce, will take about 5 minutes to be defrosted.

HEATING SAUCES BY MICROWAVE

Half a pint of thin sauces or those with sugar in will take between 1½ and 2 minutes. Half a pint of thick sauce will take 2½ to 3 minutes. Stir well before serving. Egg-based sauces should be heated slowly and the oven checked every 15 to 30 seconds.

White Sauce (coating consistency)

1 oz flour
1 oz butter
½ pint milk
seasoning

Heat the milk in the oven for 2 minutes. Melt the butter in a separate container for 1 minute. Stir the flour into the butter and cook for 1 minute. Remove from oven and gradually pour the milk into the flour mix, stirring well. Return to oven for 1½ minutes, stir or whisk and cook for a further 1 minute. Season to taste. Stir well before serving. Extra ingredients, *e.g.* parsley and cheese, should be added to the sauce with the seasoning and returned to the oven for a further 1 minute.

For a thinner sauce less flour and fat should be used; for a thicker sauce increase the amounts. Timings will be altered correspondingly.

Curry Sauce

1 oz fat
1 large onion, finely chopped
1 tablespoon curry powder
1 level tablespoon flour
½ pint stock
2 tablespoons chutney
½ teaspoon garlic salt
pinch Cayenne pepper

Place the onion with the fat in the oven for 6 minutes. Add the flour and curry powder to the onion, mix well and cook for 2 minutes. Gradually pour in the stock, mix until smooth and cook in the oven for 3 minutes. Add all other ingredients, season to taste and cook covered in the oven for 10 minutes. Stir once or twice during this cycle. Stir on removal from oven, check seasoning and allow to stand for 10 minutes before serving. Heat as required.

Gravy

1 oz meat dripping
½ pint meat or vegetable stock
1 heaped dessertspoon flour
1 level dessertspoon gravy mix
seasoning

Heat the stock for 2 minutes. Melt the dripping in the oven for 1 minute, add to it the flour and gravy mix, stir well and heat for 30 seconds. Pour in the liquid stock, mix to a smooth paste and heat in the oven for 4 minutes. Stir briskly halfway through this cycle. Season as required before serving.

Apple Sauce

8 oz cooking apples
½ oz butter
sugar to taste

Peel, core and slice the apples. Place in a covered container in the oven with 1 tablespoon of water. Cook in the microwave oven for 5 minutes (this timing will vary slightly with the type of apple used, but they should be soft when removed from the oven). Remove from oven and stir until smooth, add the butter and sugar, and mix well. Stand covered for 5 minutes before using.

Hollandaise

2 tablespoons wine vinegar
1 tablespoon water
2 egg yolks
4 oz butter
seasoning

Heat the water and vinegar together in the oven for 3 minutes. Stir the butter into the vinegar and beat well. Add the egg yolks and whisk until the ingredients are combined together. Heat in the oven for 45 seconds and whisk in the seasoning; if not quite thick enough, return to the oven for a further 15 to 30 seconds. Stand covered for 2 minutes before serving. Care must be taken when reheating this sauce as the egg will curdle if it is boiled.

Bread Sauce

2 cloves
1 medium onion, peeled
a few peppercorns
salt
¾ pint milk
3 oz white breadcrumbs

Heat the milk with the peppercorns and onion stuck with cloves for 3½ minutes. Stand to one side for 20 minutes. Remove the peppercorns, add the breadcrumbs and butter, and heat in the oven for 10 minutes. Stir once during this cycle. Remove the onion, add salt to taste, stir and allow to stand before serving.

Chocolate Sauce for Ice-cream

2 oz plain dark chocolate
1 tablespoon milk
½ oz butter

Break the chocolate into a bowl with the butter. Heat in the oven for 1 minute. Add the milk, stir until smooth and serve. This sauce can be heated gently as required.

Custard

2 tablespoons custard powder
1 tablespoon sugar
1 pint milk

Mix sugar, powder and a little of the milk to a smooth paste. Heat the remainder of the milk in the oven for 3½ minutes. Pour on to the custard powder, stirring well. Return to the oven for 2 minutes. Stir before serving.

Egg Custard Sauce

1 tablespoon sugar
2 large eggs
½ pint milk
1 teaspoon grated lemon rind

Heat the milk and lemon rind in the oven for 2 minutes. Whisk the eggs and sugar lightly together. Pour the milk on to the eggs, stir, strain the custard and place in the oven for 2½ to 3 minutes. Whisk well twice during this cycle. Leave to stand a few minutes before serving.

Meat and Poultry

Meat cooked in the oven retains all its natural juice and flavour. The oven is easy to clean after the cooking, too. Large joints of meat will colour in the oven quite successfully, but chops, steak, etc., will need to be browned after cooking or cooked in a browning dish.

HINTS FOR SUCCESSFUL MEAT COOKERY

1 After defrosting joints of meat in the oven, it is advisable to allow 30 minutes' rest before cooking.

2 For best cooking results, meat should be at room temperature rather than refrigerated.

3 Cheaper cuts of meat should be marinated before cooking.

4 Casseroles and joints of meat after cooking in the oven should be allowed to stand for at least 20 minutes before serving.

5 Stir casseroles during the cooking cycle.

6 Turn joints of meat over during the cooking cycle.

7 If the family is divided on the degree to which meat should be cooked, cut the joint after standing time and place part back into the oven for further cooking.

8 Always cook joints and poultry on a roasting rack.

DEFROSTING MEAT BY MICROWAVE

For even defrosting of meat it is important that the meat is as even in shape as possible. Mince, liver, kidneys, etc., should be gently separated halfway through the defrosting cycle. Use the defrost switch if fitted; if not see page 40 for timings.

Food	Time
Lamb chops, 8 oz	2 mins
Liver, 1 lb	2 mins; separate 2 mins

Food	Time
Mince beef, 8 oz	3 mins; separate 3 mins
Steak, 2 × 6 oz	3 mins; separate 2 mins
Joints of meat per lb	5 mins
Chicken per lb	6 mins

REHEATING MEAT BY MICROWAVE

Cover any meat or meat dishes to be heated in the oven. Sliced meat should be moistened with a little of the meat juices or gravy before heating. Family-size pasta dishes should be turned during the heating process. Casseroles should be stirred.

Food	Time
Lasagne, 12 oz	4 mins
Casserole, 1 portion	1½ mins
Family-size casserole	4–5 mins
Sliced meat, 1 portion	45 secs
Chicken, 3 lb	6 mins
Chicken portion	1¼ mins

COOKING MEAT BY MICROWAVE

Before cooking a joint of meat it should be seasoned. If it is an uneven shape – *e.g.* leg of lamb – bone and roll, or place a thin piece of foil around the narrow end. This will prevent the part covered from overcooking by reflecting the waves away. Remove the foil after half the cooking time has elapsed.

The meat can be cooked by two different methods in the oven. Either cook it on defrost power, or use the stand-and-wait method. By the latter method the joint is placed in the oven for half the cooking time, then allowed to rest for 15 minutes and returned to the oven for the rest of the time. Meat cooked by either method can be wrapped in foil for 20 minutes before carving. Use a roasting bag for cooking the meat in, but never use a metal tag – leave it open. The meat can be placed under the grill during the resting time to crispen the skin or give further colouring. It is advisable to check the temperature of the meat with a meat thermometer. Remove from the oven when the temperature registers 15°F below the final temperature required. *Do not leave the thermometer in the oven during the cooking cycle.*

Meat	Timing per lb on defrost (mins)	Timing per lb full power (mins)		Temperature after standing (Fahrenheit)
Beef	7	Rare	5	140°
	8	Medium	6	160°
	10	Well done	7	170°
Pork	12		8	185°
Lamb	10		6½	175°
Veal	10		6½	170°
Chicken	8		5	185°
Turkey	8		5½	185°

Note: The wings and ends of legs of chicken should be wrapped in foil for half the cooking time. Sprinkle chicken with a chicken seasoning or paprika before cooking to increase the colour.

A whole chicken cooked in the microwave oven is shown in illustration 3 in the colour section.

Bacon Slices and Gammon Steaks

These can be cooked in the microwave oven. The longer they are left in the oven, the browner and crisper they will become. The rind of the bacon or gammon should be snipped before cooking. Place the bacon on a sheet of absorbent paper. An 8 oz gammon steak will take about 2½ minutes to cook, two rashers of bacon about 2 minutes.

Hamburgers, Chops, Liver, Kidneys, etc.

All of these small meat items can be cooked in the oven but will require browning before cooking. This can be done in a frying pan or under the grill. Brush with soy sauce and season, place on a plate, cover and cook. The timing is about 2 minutes per lb, depending on personal taste.

DEFROST CONTROL

In some of the following recipes defrost power is used, as it is ideal for meat cookery. Where there is no defrost control on the oven, the dish can be cooked on full power using 75 per cent of the time recommended.

Lamb Chops

4 lamb chops
1 onion, sliced
4 slices lemon
½ green pepper, thinly sliced
½ lb tomatoes
2 fl oz stock
salt and pepper
1 teaspoon chopped parsley

Place the chops in a dish. Place the lemon slice on top of the chops. Cover with all the other ingredients. Season, cover and cook in the oven for 16 minutes on defrost control. Stand for 5 minutes covered before serving.

Paprika Chicken

1½ lb chicken pieces, skin removed
flour
3 teaspoons paprika
caraway seeds
¼ lb button mushrooms
½ pint chicken stock
small carton soured cream
salt and pepper

Toss the chicken pieces in the flour and fry in a frying pan until brown. Remove the chicken from the pan. Mix the paprika with a little water to form a thick paste. Spread this over the chicken. Place the chicken, mushrooms, stock and a few caraway seeds into a casserole dish. Cook on defrost for 22 minutes. Stir once during this cycle. Check the seasoning, and just before serving pour on the soured cream.

Cottage Pie

12 oz cooked meat, finely minced
1 onion, chopped
¼ pint stock
½ oz margarine
seasoning
1 lb mashed potatoes

Melt the margarine in the oven for 1 minute; sauté the onion for 2 minutes. Mix with the meat and stock. Season to taste. Place in a dish and cover with the potato. Cook in the oven for 15 minutes. Turn twice during this cycle. Place under the grill to brown before serving.

Spicy Meat Loaf
See illustration 4 in colour section

1 lb minced beef
1 medium chopped onion
4 oz chopped mushrooms
½ oz margarine
1 egg
½ teaspoon salt
1 tablespoon potato powder
1 teaspoon dried parsley
1 teaspoon curry powder
1 teaspoon soy sauce
1 dessertspoon Worcester sauce

Cook the mushrooms and onion in the margarine for 4 minutes in the oven. Drain off the fat and mix well together with all the other ingredients. Shape into a loaf on a shallow cooking dish. Cover with greaseproof paper and cook in the oven for 6 minutes.
For the sauce: Mix together 1 heaped dessertspoon soft dark-brown sugar, 1½ teaspoons mustard powder, 1 teaspoon soy sauce, 3 tablespoons chutney and 1 teaspoon curry powder. Spoon the sauce over the meat loaf and cook uncovered in the oven for a further 7 minutes. Leave to stand for 10 minutes before serving.

Chicken à la King

8 oz cooked chicken, diced
½ green pepper, sliced
½ red pepper, sliced
3 oz mushrooms, sliced
1 oz butter
1 oz flour
¾ pint milk and chicken stock, mixed
salt, pepper and nutmeg

Melt the butter for 1 minute and sauté the mushrooms and peppers for 6 minutes. Stir in the flour and mix well. Heat the stock in the oven for 3 minutes. Gradually add the stock to the flour, stirring well. Return the container to the oven for 5 minutes. Stir once during this cycle. Add the chicken and seasoning, return to the oven for 6 minutes, stir and garnish with parsley before serving.

Devilled Kidneys

8 lamb's kidneys, sliced
1 oz margarine
1 small onion, finely chopped
salt and pepper
1 tablespoon Worcester sauce
1 tablespoon dry sherry
1 tablespoon finely chopped parsley

Melt the margarine in the oven for 1 minute, sauté the onion for 2 minutes. Add the seasoning and the kidneys, cook for 2 minutes, stir and cook for a further 2 minutes. Add the sherry, Worcester sauce and parsley, and cook for 2 minutes. Garnish with croûtons before serving.

Savoury Mince

8 oz raw minced beef
½ oz butter
1 chopped onion
2 chopped carrots
2 oz chopped mushrooms
½ pint beef stock
1 dessertspoon parsley, chopped
½ teaspoon celery salt
1 dessertspoon tomato purée
1 tablespoon porridge oats
pepper and salt

Heat the butter in the oven for 45 seconds, sauté the carrots and onions for 3 minutes. Mix in the mushrooms and the minced meat; cook for a further 3 minutes. Add all other ingredients except for the salt and pepper, cover and cook for 24 minutes on defrost power. Remove from the oven and check the seasoning. Leave to stand for 10 minutes before serving.

Pork Chops with Pineapple

4 pork chops
4 pineapple rings
4 teaspoons soft brown sugar
¼ pint chicken stock
1 oz butter
5 fl oz soured cream

Season chops and colour in frying pan. Place in dish suitable for the oven, place the pineapple rings on top and sprinkle with the sugar. Pour the stock around the chops and cook covered in the oven on defrost for 6 minutes. Remove the chops and heat the liquid at full power for 4 minutes, add the soured cream and stir. Serve the chops with the sauce poured over.

Curry

12 oz cooked meat
2 tablespoons coconut
1 tablespoon water
1 onion, chopped
1 apple, peeled, cored and sliced
1 oz margarine
1 tablespoon curry powder
2 oz flour
¾ pint stock
2 oz sultanas
1 tablespoon tomato purée
½ teaspoon sugar
½ teaspoon salt
1 tablespoon lemon juice

Heat the coconut in the water for 2 minutes. Heat the margarine for 1 minute. Sauté the onion and the apple for 3 minutes. Add the flour and curry, mix well, heat in the oven for 1 minute and gradually add the stock, stirring well. Add all other ingredients, stir, cover and heat for 12 minutes. Stir once during this cycle. Stand for 5 minutes before serving.

Chicken Favourite

4 chicken breasts, skinned
2 oz flaked almonds
4 slices bacon
1 × 10½ fl oz can condensed cream of chicken soup
2 tablespoons sherry.

Spread the almonds out on a shallow dish. Heat in the oven until brown, about 5 minutes. Cook bacon between layers of absorbent paper for 2 minutes in the oven. Wrap a piece of bacon around each chicken breast. Cook covered in the oven for 12 to 15 minutes (until cooked). Drain the juices from the chicken and mix with the soup and sherry. Pour the sauce over the chicken and heat for a further 5 minutes covered in the oven. Top with the almonds before serving.

Fish

If fish is not your favourite food to cook, try using it in the microwave oven. The first thing you will notice is that there is no 'fishy smell' throughout the kitchen; then you will see how firm the texture is and how good the colour, and the taste is moist and full of flavour. The dish used for cooking is so much easier to clean, too. Fish will soon become a firm favourite with you and your family.

HINTS FOR SUCCESSFUL FISH COOKERY

1 Generally fish is cooked covered.
2 Fish cooks very quickly in the microwave oven, so undertime rather than overtime.
3 Fish will carry on cooking while standing. If adding a sauce, remove the fish before completion of cooking.
4 Always brush the skin of fish with a little melted fat before cooking, as it may sometimes dry in the oven.
5 When the fish is enclosed with a skin, *e.g.* trout, make a couple of slits in the skin to let steam escape.
6 When cooking large whole fish in the oven, wrap a thin piece of foil around the tail end to prevent overcooking. Remove the foil halfway through the cooking cycle.
7 When cooking thin fillets of fish, overlap the tail ends to prevent overcooking.
8 The thickest parts of the fish should be placed towards the edge of the container.

DEFROSTING FISH BY MICROWAVE

Fish defrosts very quickly in the microwave oven, as it is even in its bone structure and general composition. Keep the fish covered during defrosting and turn over once during the cycle. When defrosting prawns, etc., place in a covered container and shake at intervals.

Food	Time
Cod steak, 3½ oz	2 mins; rest before using
Prawns, 8 oz	4 mins
Trout, 7 oz	2½ mins
Fish, 1 lb	6 mins; rest before using

HEATING FISH BY MICROWAVE

The fish that is to be heated should be kept covered except for breaded items, which should be placed on absorbent paper before being heated.

Food	Time
Portion of fish fingers	1 min
1 lb fried fish	3 mins
1 lb fish in sauce	4 mins

Smoked Haddock

8 oz smoked haddock
½ oz butter
2 tablespoons milk

Grease dish lightly, place the fish into it, pour over the milk and dot with butter. Cook covered in the microwave oven for 4 minutes. Remove, cover and serve. This timing will alter slightly depending on the temperature and shape of the fish.

Crispy Cod

2 cod cutlets
¾ oz butter
salt and pepper
2 rashers bacon
small handful of potato crisps

Place the cod cutlets on a dish, dot with the butter and sprinkle with the seasoning. Cover and cook in the oven for 4 minutes. Remove cover and baste with the juices made during cooking. Return to the oven covered for a further 2 minutes. Remove from the oven and stand to one side covered. Cook the bacon on absorbent paper in the oven for 2 to 3 minutes until crisp. Crumble the bacon over the fish and sprinkle with the crushed potato crisps. If this dish is made in advance to be heated later, heat uncovered so that the bacon and crisps stay firm.

Haddock with Prawns
See illustration 5 in colour section

4 pieces haddock
4 oz prawns, peeled
½ pint water
1 oz butter
1 red pepper sliced
6 oz sliced mushrooms
seasoning
small can sweetcorn

Skin the haddock, place the skin in the water and heat in the oven for 5 minutes. Leave to stand. Heat the butter for 1 minute and add the onions, pepper and mushrooms. Sauté in the oven for 5 minutes. Stir once during this cycle. Drain the fish skin from the water. Add the water and seasoning to the vegetables and lay the fish on top. Cover and cook for 5 minutes. Add to the fish the prawns and sweetcorn. Cover and cook for a further 3 minutes. Serve hot, garnished with parsley.

Red Mullet with Tomatoes

2 red mullets, cleaned
½ medium onion, finely chopped
small tin tomatoes
garlic salt
½ oz butter
black pepper
1 teaspoon lemon juice
chopped parsley

Melt the butter in the oven for 1 minute; sauté the onions in the butter for 2½ minutes. Place the fish on top of the

1 A succulent steak cooked in the microwave browning dish

2 Three nutritious soups — lettuce, tomato and cream of corn

3 A roast chicken cooked in the microwave oven

4 Spicy meat loaf

5 Haddock with prawns

6 Sweet and sour prawns with rice

7 Blackcurrant flan and apple fool

8 Chocolate gâteau

onions and cover with the tomatoes, lemon juice and a sprinkle of garlic salt and pepper. Cover and cook for 7 to 8 minutes. Before serving, sprinkle with the chopped parsley. This dish can be served either hot or cold.

Prawn Paste

9 oz cod
8 oz butter
8 oz prawns
½ teaspoon mace
1 teaspoon paprika
salt
1 teaspoon lemon juice

Cook the cod in a covered dish for 6 minutes. Remove from the oven and pound well. Mix the prawns with the fish. Soften the butter in the oven for 1 minute and add to the fish with the lemon juice and seasoning. Mix well and heat in the oven for 3 minutes. Put into a shallow dish and leave to set. When cool, cover with a thin layer of clarified butter and garnish with sliced stuffed olives. Leave in the refrigerator for 2 hours before serving. Serve with salad and toast or brown bread.
Note: The butter can be clarified by heating in the oven for several minutes and then straining.

Salmon Layer Crisp

1 × 7½ oz can salmon
1 oz butter
1 oz flour
½ pint milk including liquor from salmon
1 dessertspoon lemon juice
1 egg yolk
seasoning
5 oz breadcrumbs
3 oz butter

Melt 1 oz of butter in the oven for 1 minute. Add the flour and mix well, then return to the oven for 40 seconds. Heat the milk for 2 minutes, gradually stir into the flour and mix until smooth. Return to the oven for 2 minutes. Stir in the lemon juice, egg yolk, seasoning and flaked salmon. Cook for 2 minutes. Stir and stand covered to one side. Heat the 3 oz of butter in the oven for 3 minutes. Mix in the breadcrumbs, heat for 5 minutes, stir with a fork and heat for a further 5 minutes or until brown. Stir on removal from oven. Place a layer of the breadcrumbs mix into a dish, cover with the salmon mix and top with the breadcrumbs. Heat in the oven for 3 minutes.

Sweet and Sour Prawns
See illustration 6 in colour section

1 dessertspoon soy sauce
2 flat tablespoons cornflour
3 tablespoons soft dark-brown sugar
½ teaspoon ginger
1 teaspoon paprika
3 tablespoons vinegar
1 can pineapple pieces
1 dessertspoon redcurrant jelly
8 oz prawns
1 small onion, chopped
1 green pepper, thinly sliced
1 carrot, cut into thin strips
4 tablespoons water

In a casserole dish combine the soy sauce, cornflour, sugar, ginger, paprika, vinegar, juice from pineapple, redcurrant jelly and water. Place in the oven and heat for 1 minute. Stir well. Add the carrots, onion and peppers. Cover and cook for 6 minutes. Stir once during this cycle. Add the prawns and pineapple pieces, cover and heat for a further 5 minutes. Stir well before serving.

Fish Pie

1 lb fish
½ pint milk
2 hard-boiled eggs
1 oz butter
1 oz flour
½ teaspoon celery salt
pepper
chopped parsley
1 lb mashed potatoes

Cook the fish covered in the oven for 5 minutes. Remove and stand to one side. Melt the butter in the oven for 1 minute. Stir in the flour and cook for 40 seconds. Heat the milk for 2 minutes and gradually add to the flour, stirring well. Return to the oven for 1 minute. Mix well. Flake the fish and add with the seasoning, parsley and chopped hard-boiled eggs to the milk. Line a dish with the mashed potatoes, pour the fish into the centre and heat for 6 minutes in the oven. Remove from oven and place under the grill to brown just before serving.

Trout Rosé

2 medium trout, cleaned
1 oz butter
½ small onion, finely chopped
¼ pint rosé wine
4 dessertspoons hollandaise sauce
salt and pepper
croûtons
parsley

Note: For the making of the hollandaise sauce, turn to the section on sauces and make this before cooking the fish.
Place trout in a shallow dish. Add the wine, sprinkle with the onions and dot with butter. Cook covered in the oven for 5 minutes. Remove the trout from the stock. Skin the fish carefully. Heat the stock for 3 minutes, add 3

tablespoons to the hollandaise sauce and mix well. Return the trout to the oven for 1¾ minutes. Pour the sauce over the trout and heat for a further 45 seconds. Garnish with the croûtons and parsley.

Haddock Fillets with Oregano

12 oz haddock fillets
1 oz breadcrumbs
1 heaped teaspoon dried oregano
1 oz butter
1 tablespoon seedless raisins
1 tablespoon water
salt and pepper
4 slices lemon

Lay the fish in a shallow dish, add the water and dot with butter. Mix the breadcrumbs with the seasoning and oregano; sprinkle over the fish. Cover and cook in the oven for 4 minutes. Add the raisins and lemon slices to the fish. Return to the oven covered for a further 2 minutes. Garnish with parsley and serve hot.

Creamy Tuna Fish

1 oz butter
1 oz flour
¼ red pepper, finely chopped
1 × 7 oz can tuna fish
1 dessertspoon capers, rinsed and chopped
12 black olives, stoned and chopped
½ pint milk
salt and pepper

Melt the butter in the oven for 1 minute and sauté the peppers for 2 minutes. Stir in the flour and mix well. Return to the oven for 1 minute. Slowly add the milk, stirring well until smooth. Cook in the oven for 3 minutes. Stir well and add the seasoning, flaked tuna fish, olives and capers. Cook covered in the oven for 4 minutes. Stir and serve on hot toast as a snack or starter to a meal.

Vegetables

When vegetables are cooked by microwave, whether fresh or frozen, the full flavour and colour remains to be tasted and admired. Less nutritional value is lost during the cooking process also. Even reheated vegetables taste and look freshly cooked. When using canned vegetables, just open the can, drain the vegetables into a serving dish, add a knob of butter and heat covered until hot. Cooking of vegetables in the oven is not always quicker than by conventional means, but the results are superior. Try for yourself and see.

HINTS FOR SUCCESSFUL VEGETABLE COOKERY

1 Always cover the vegetables during a cooking or heating cycle.
2 Do not add salt until after the vegetables are cooked, as it tends to dry the food during the cooking process.
3 Best results are achieved by keeping the vegetables even in size.
4 Most vegetables will need to be stirred in their dish once during the cooking cycle.
5 Standing time for vegetables after cooking is between 2 and 5 minutes.
6 Covered dishes of vegetables will keep hot for up to 10 minutes after removing from the oven.
7 With irregular-shaped vegetables, *e.g.* broccoli, place the thickest parts near to the edge of the dish.
8 Flat, shallow dishes are more successful than deep ones for cooking vegetables.
Note: When removing the cover or lid from a dish, take care not to be burnt by steam.

FROZEN VEGETABLES AND MICROWAVE

All frozen vegetables can be cooked straight from the frozen condition in the oven. The following timings have been given for 8 oz weight in all cases.

Vegetable	Water/Method	Cooking time
Asparagus	4 tbs	8 mins + 5 standing
Broccoli	4 tbs	8 mins + 5 standing
Beans	4 tbs	5 mins + 3 standing
Broad beans	4 tbs	8 mins + 3 standing
Cauliflower	4 tbs	8 mins + 3 standing
Carrots, whole	4 tbs	8 mins + 2 standing
Corn	2 tbs	5 mins + 2 standing
Corn-on-the-cob	Wrap in greaseproof paper	5 mins + 1 standing
Mixed veg	2 tbs	5 mins + 2 standing
Peas	½ oz butter	5 mins + 2 standing

FRESH VEGETABLES AND MICROWAVE

The timings will vary on fresh vegetables, depending on the age, size and freshness. All timings in the following table are for 8 oz weight, except in the case of potatoes (1 lb).

Vegetable	Water/Method	Cooking time
Beans	6 tbs	6–7 mins
Broad beans	4 tbs	8 mins + 2 standing
Beetroot	6 tbs	12 mins + 5 standing
Cabbage	2 tbs	6 mins + 5 standing
Cauliflower	6 tbs	9 mins + 3 standing
Celery	4 tbs	10–15 mins + 3 standing
Corn-on-the-cob	Wrap in greaseproof paper	4–5 mins + 2 standing
Onions, whole	No additions	4 mins + 2 standing
Potatoes, boiled (1 lb)	6 tbs	10 mins + 5 standing
Peas	4 tbs	9 mins + 3 standing
Tomatoes, halved	Dot with butter	3 mins
Mushrooms	1 oz fat	4 mins

To serve, drain the vegetables and season. Dot with butter and garnish if required.

54

HEATING VEGETABLES BY MICROWAVE

All vegetables to be heated in the oven should be covered.

Food	Time
Rice, 8 oz	2 mins; fork before serving
One portion of vegetables	30 secs–1 min
Four portions of vegetables	2 mins–2½ mins

Rice

8 oz long-grain patna rice
1¾ pt boiling water

Place the rice in a large bowl and pour over the boiling water. Cook covered in the oven for 16 minutes. Season and leave to stand for 5 minutes before serving.

Cauliflower Polonaise

1 medium-sized cauliflower
1 hard-boiled egg
1 oz butter
1 oz breadcrumbs
seasoning

Cook the cauliflower with 8 tablespoons of water for 8 minutes in a covered dish in the oven. Drain, season and keep covered. Chop finely the white of the egg and rub the yolk through a sieve. Melt the butter in the oven for 1 minute, toss in the breadcrumbs and cook until brown, approximately 3 minutes. Stir every minute. Garnish the cauliflower with the breadcrumbs, egg white and yolk before serving.

Stuffed Peppers

4 peppers
8 oz mince
1 onion, chopped
2 oz chopped mushrooms
1 tablespoon tomato purée
2 oz breadcrumbs
salt and pepper
1 teaspoon marjoram

Slice the top of the peppers and remove the inside. Place the peppers in a dish with 4 tablespoons of water and cook covered in the oven for 4 minutes. Place the minced beef in the oven and heat for 3 minutes. Stir, add the chopped onion and mushrooms, and heat for 2 minutes. Add the tomato purée, breadcrumbs, salt and pepper, and herbs. Fill the peppers, place in a dish and moisten with a little beef stock. Cook covered for 15 minutes. Stand for 5 minutes before serving.

Bavarian Red Cabbage

12 oz red cabbage, finely shredded
1 large cooking apple, peeled and sliced
1 small onion, stuck with cloves
2 tablespoons lemon juice
1 oz margarine
1 teaspoon cornflour
1 bayleaf
1 tablespoon sugar
pinch of cinnamon
¾ pint stock

Melt the margarine in the oven for 1 minute. Toss the cabbage in the margarine. Cook covered for 8 minutes. Add the onion, bayleaf, lemon juice, sugar and cinnamon. Stir and heat covered for 5 minutes. Add the stock and apple. Cook covered for 12 minutes. Remove the onion and bayleaf, mix the cornflour with a little water and stir

into the cabbage. Cook covered for a further 5 minutes.
Stir before serving.

Savoury Vegetable Flan

1 pre-baked flan case
1 small onion, finely chopped
garlic salt
½ oz butter
1 oz breadcrumbs
1 egg
¼ pint double cream
1 small green pepper, thinly sliced
4 tomatoes, skinned and chopped
1 oz grated cheese

Melt the butter in the microwave for 45 seconds. Sauté the
onion and peppers for 5 minutes. Beat the egg with the
cream and stir in the breadcrumbs, tomatoes, seasoning
and cheese. Place the onions and pepper in the base of the
flan and cover with the cream mix. Cook in the oven for 6
minutes. Turn the flan once during this cycle. Let it stand
before serving and garnish with sliced tomatoes and
parsley.

Savoury Mushrooms

8 large button mushrooms
1 oz breadcrumbs
1 oz Stilton cheese
1 oz butter

Remove the stems from the mushrooms and chop finely.
Melt the butter in the oven for 1 minute. Sauté the
chopped stems for 1½ minutes. Mix in the breadcrumbs
and crumbled Stilton. Mix well. Fill the mushrooms and
cook in the oven for 2 to 3 minutes. Sprinkle with chopped
parsley before serving.

Broad Beans in Tomato Sauce

12 oz cooked broad beans
1 tablespoon oil
1 small onion, finely chopped
small can tomatoes
1 teaspoon tomato purée
2 tablespoons water
¼ teaspoon sugar
salt and pepper

Melt the oil in the oven for 30 seconds, sauté the onion for 2 minutes, add all other ingredients and cook for 5 minutes covered. Stir well and return to the oven for 2 minutes uncovered. Pour over the broad beans and heat in the oven covered for 3 minutes. Stir before serving and garnish with parsley.

Stuffed Tomatoes

4 large tomatoes
1 small onion, finely chopped
2 oz bacon, finely chopped
1½ oz breadcrumbs
1 oz butter
salt and pepper

Cut the top off the tomatoes, scoop out the inside and chop. Heat the butter in the oven for 45 seconds, add the onion and bacon, and sauté for 2½ minutes. Add the breadcrumbs, seasoning and tomato flesh, stir and heat for 1 minute. Fill the tomatoes and cover with the tops. Cook in the oven for 4 minutes. Stand 1 minute before serving.

Caramelled Potatoes

1 lb small potatoes
1½ oz soft brown sugar
1 oz butter
1 tablespoon water

Cook the potatoes in a covered container with 6 tablespoons of water for 7 minutes, drain and stand to one side. Heat the butter, sugar and water together in the oven for 5 minutes. Stir well and add the potatoes. Turn in the sugar, cook for 6 minutes, gently stirring the potatoes every 2 minutes.

Baked Tomatoes

½ lb sliced tomatoes
1 medium onion, finely sliced
3 oz breadcrumbs
2 oz grated cheese
seasoning
chopped parsley

Melt the margarine in the oven for 30 seconds. Sauté the onions for 3½ minutes. Mix the onions with the breadcrumbs and the cheese. Place a layer of the tomatoes in a greased dish, season lightly and cover with some of the breadcrumb mix. Carry on with the layering, finishing with the breadcrumbs. Cook covered for 5 minutes. Cover the dish with the remaining cheese and return the dish to the oven for a further 2 minutes. Sprinkle with the crushed cereal and parsley before serving.

Jacket Potato

1 medium-sized potato
butter
salt and pepper

Clean and dry the potato, wrap in absorbent paper, place in the oven and cook for about 5½ minutes. Turn over once during the cooking cycle. Remove from the oven and wrap in aluminium foil. Leave to stand for 5 minutes. Slit the foil, open the potato, season and add a knob of butter before serving.

Fruit

Fruit and microwave – my favourite combination. Fruit when cooked in the oven retains all its original flavour, colour and taste, even when cooking for a puréed state. Fruit dishes are perfect for reheating, too, so you can always prepare these in advance of requirements. Take care when adding sugar to a recipe, as generally less is required than with conventional cooking methods.

HINTS FOR SUCCESSFUL FRUIT COOKERY
1   The timing will vary slightly depending on the variety of fruit being cooked, so do check by opening the oven door and testing. The end result will not be affected.
2   Take fruit out of the oven just before it is cooked. Standing time is part of the cooking time.
3   When preparing the fruit for cooking, even-sized pieces make for easier cooking.
4   Generally fruit should be covered during the cooking cycle. For maximum flavour most of the recipes recommend a little water being added. Keep the fruit covered during the standing cycle, too.
5   Before squeezing oranges and lemons place them in the oven for a few seconds and see how much more juice you get from them.
6   For easier peeling and skinning of fruit, place in the oven to heat slightly before starting.

DEFROSTING FRUIT BY MICROWAVE
If there are any apparent ice crystals on the outside of the fruit, brush them off before defrosting. The fruits should be rearranged halfway through the defrosting cycle, so stir

gently. Keep the fruit covered, except for strawberries, which are better defrosted uncovered.

One pound of fruit will take approximately 3 minutes to defrost. Let the fruit stand before using.

HEATING FRUIT BY MICROWAVE

When heating fruit by microwave, keep the item covered. With poached or stewed fruit, stir gently before serving.

One fruit portion will take between 45 seconds and 1 minute to heat.

Poached Fruit

1 lb sliced apples
¼ lb sugar
2 tablespoons water
lemon juice

Place all the ingredients into a shallow dish and cook covered for about 8 minutes. Stir once during this cycle. Allow to stand before serving.

Blackcurrants

8 oz blackcurrants
3 oz caster sugar
1 tablespoon water

Place all the ingredients into a compact dish and cook covered in the oven for 5 minutes. Stand covered before serving.

Plums

1 lb plums
4 oz caster sugar
1 tablespoon water

Place all the ingredients into a dish. Cook covered in the oven for 5 minutes, stir and stand before serving.

Pears

1 lb pears, sliced
4 oz sugar
¼ pint water
lemon juice

Place all the ingredients into a shallow dish. Cook covered for 10 minutes. Allow to stand covered for 5 minutes before serving.

Apple Fool
See illustration 7 in colour section

2 lb cooking apples
4 oz sugar
½ pint double cream
green colouring

Peel, core and slice the apples. Place in a covered dish with the sugar for 17 minutes. Stir twice during this cooking cycle. Allow the apples to cool on removal from the oven. Purée the apples. Whip the cream lightly and fold into the apples. Colour half the mix with the green colouring and place in layers into four serving glasses. Serve chilled, garnished with angelica.

Stuffed Peaches

3 good-sized ripe peaches
1 oz sponge cake crumbs
1 oz ground almonds
1 oz caster sugar
2 tablespoons medium dry sherry
demerara sugar

Place the sponge cake crumbs, ground almonds and caster sugar in a bowl. Add the sherry and mix well. Heat the whole peaches in the oven for 45 seconds, allow to cool and gently remove the skins. Cut the peaches in half, remove the stone and place in a shallow dish. Pile the stuffing into the stone cavities and sprinkle with the demerara sugar. Place in the oven uncovered and cook for 6 minutes. Turn the dish once during this cycle. Garnish with blanched almonds and cherries. Serve hot or cold with cream.

Baked Apples

4 cooking apples, cored
4 tablespoons demerara sugar
1 oz butter
2 tablespoons sweet cider
For the sauce:
2 level tablespoons demerara sugar
cider
flaked almonds

Place the apples in a shallow dish, fill each with 1 tablespoon of sugar and top with ¼ oz butter. Pour the 2 tablespoons of cider into the base of the dish. Cover and cook in the oven for 4 to 5 minutes, depending on the type of apple. Remove the apples from the syrup. Make up the syrup to 5 fl oz with the additional cider. Heat the syrup with the sugar in the oven for 5 minutes. Stir twice carefully during this cycle. Pour the syrup over the apples and serve, garnished with the almonds.

Pears with Chocolate Sauce

3 large pears, peeled and quartered
1 tablespoon caster sugar
3 tablespoons water
4 oz plain dark chocolate
vanilla essence

Cook the pears in a covered container with the water, sugar and a few drops of vanilla essence for 3 minutes. Stir and return covered to the oven for a further 3 minutes. Drain the juice from the pears. Break the chocolate into the juice and heat in the oven for 1¼ minutes. Stir well and pour over the pears. Heat uncovered in the oven for 2 minutes and stir. Leave to stand uncovered for 5 minutes before serving.

Lemon Meringue Pie

2 lemons, grated and squeezed
2 tablespoons cornflour
6 oz caster sugar
2 eggs separated
water
1 biscuit crust flan

Make the lemon juice up to half a pint with the water. Blend the cornflour with the water, heat in the oven with the grated rind, butter and 3 oz of the sugar for 2 minutes, stir and return to the oven for a further 2 minutes. Stir well on removal. Allow to cool slightly and add the egg yolks, mix well, heat for 2 minutes in the oven and pour the lemon mix into the flan case. Beat the egg whites until stiff and fold in the remaining sugar. Pile the meringue on to the lemon and place under the grill to brown. Serve hot or cold.

Cinnamon Apples

4 eating apples, quartered and cored
1½ oz butter
1 tablespoon demerara sugar
1 teaspoon cinammon

Heat the butter in the oven for 1½ minutes. Toss the apples in the butter and heat for 1 minute. Toss the apples again and heat for a further 1 minute. Sprinkle with the sugar and cinnamon, stir gently and heat for 1 minute. Stir before serving. Serve hot with ice-cream or cream.

Desserts

The microwave oven certainly comes into its own when a quick sweet is needed to finish off a meal. Most of the recipes suggested can be left to cook while you are eating, or of course can be prepared in advance and heated as required. Sponge-based sweets will be paler than normal in colouring, but, if served with a sauce, look attractive and taste delicious.

HINTS FOR SUCCESSFUL DESSERTS

1   Cover sponge-based items with a cooking film, or top the bowl with a plate. Be careful on removing the cover as steam will have collected underneath.
2   Use a large container for milk-based sweets to guard against boiling over.
3   Remember to turn the cooking container during the cycle for an even end result.
4   Leave the desserts to stand for a few minutes before serving.

DEFROSTING FROZEN DESSERTS BY MICROWAVE

Care must be taken when defrosting sweets with jelly or cream as part of their ingredients. Increase the time by 50 per cent when defrosting more than one portion.

Food	Time
Pancakes (2)	30 secs
Mousse	20 secs
Fruit trifles	30 secs
Fruit flan	1 min

HEATING DESSERTS BY MICROWAVE

Where jam or a sugary syrup is on the dessert, be careful
not to overheat as the sugar content heats rapidly.

Food	Time
Pancakes (2)	20 secs
Apple turnover	40 secs
Sponge pudding and custard	1 min; keep covered
Christmas pudding	1½ mins per lb; keep covered
Family-size apple crumble	2½–3 mins

Spanish Dessert

4 slices fruit cake
1 can mandarin oranges
1 tablespoon sherry
1 teaspoon cornflour
½ pint milk
1 oz sugar
2 egg yolks
salt
vanilla essence

Drain the fruit, keeping the juice. Lay the cake slices into
a dish and arrange the fruit on top. Mix the juice with the
sherry and pour over the sponge. Mix the cornflour with a
little milk until smooth. Beat the egg yolks with the sugar,
pinch of salt and the rest of the milk. Stir the cornflour
into the egg/milk mix. Heat the custard in the oven for 3½
minutes, stirring every minute. Place the cake in the oven
and heat covered for 3 minutes. Return the custard to the
oven for a further ½ minute and stir well on removal from
the oven. Pour over the cake. Garnish with glacé cherries
and angelica leaves.

Creamy Semolina

1 pint milk
1½ oz semolina
1 oz butter
1 oz sugar
nutmeg

Heat the milk in a large container in the oven for 5 minutes. Stir in the semolina and cook for 3 minutes. Add the butter and sugar, stir and return to the oven for 2 minutes. To serve, sprinkle with nutmeg.

Chocolate Cream Pie

8 oz digestive biscuit crumbs
4 oz butter
½ pint milk
1 oz caster sugar
1 oz plain flour
1½ teaspoons cornflour
2 eggs
1 oz butter
3 oz plain chocolate

Grease an 8-inch flan dish. Melt the butter in the oven for 1½ minutes, stir in the biscuit crumbs and press well into the flan dish. Heat the milk in the oven for 2 minutes. Blend the sugar, flour and cornflour into a smooth paste and slowly add the milk to the egg mix. Heat in the oven, stirring every 30 seconds. Remove from the oven and stir in the chocolate. Heat for a further 45 seconds. Mix well on removal from the oven. Allow to cool slightly, spoon into a biscuit case and leave in the refrigerator to set. Decorate with cream before serving.

Quick Lemon Sponge

This sponge dessert makes its own creamy sauce.

4 oz soft brown sugar
2 oz margarine
juice and grated rind of 1 lemon
½ pint milk
2 eggs, separated
2 oz self-raising flour

Cream the sugar, margarine and lemon rind together. Add the egg yolks and beat well. Stir in the lemon juice, milk and flour. Whisk the egg whites until stiff and fold gently into the lemon mix. Pour into a greased baking dish. Stand the dish in a water bath in the microwave oven.

Cook for 10 minutes until firm to the touch; the time will tend to vary slightly depending on the amount of water placed into the water bath. On removal from the oven, place under the grill to brown the surface lightly.

Kitsgarge

6 oz Danish butter, unsalted
3 oz cocoa
9 oz icing sugar
3 tablespoons milk
1 egg yolk
7 oz plain square biscuits

Melt the butter in the microwave oven for 2 minutes. Sift the icing sugar and cocoa into the butter. Stir well and return to the oven for 1 minute. Stir and cool slightly before adding the egg yolk and milk. Line a square dish with non-stick or greased paper. Pour in a thin layer of chocolate, cover with biscuits and repeat, ending with a layer of biscuits. Place in the refrigerator for 2 hours before serving. Turn out and decorate with cream and almonds.

Pineapple Upside-down Pudding

5 oz margarine
5 oz caster sugar
6 oz self-raising flour
2 eggs
3 tablespoons milk
1 small can pineapple rings
glacé cherries
2 oz soft dark brown sugar
2 oz butter

Heat 2 oz of butter in the oven for 1 minute. Brush on to the base and sides of an 8-inch round dish. Sprinkle the 2 oz of brown sugar on to the butter and press against the dish. Place the drained pineapple rings in the base of the dish and use the cherries in between the rings. Cream the margarine and caster sugar together, beat in the eggs and fold in the flour and milk. Cover the pineapple with this mix. Even out and cover. Place in the oven for 8 minutes. Turn twice during this cycle. Allow to stand in cooking dish for 3 minutes before turning out. Serve hot or cold with cream or custard.

Sweet Pastry

7 oz plain wholemeal flour
4 oz caster sugar
1 egg
5 oz soft margarine
½ teaspoon almond essence
1 teaspoon cinnamon
2 oz ground almonds
1 dessertspoon lemon juice

Gently combine all of the ingredients together to make a soft dough. Place the dough in the refrigerator for 20 minutes. Grease a 7-inch flan dish and press half the pastry into the dish to form the flan case. Trim the edges and return covered to the refrigerator for 20 minutes. The remaining pastry will keep in the fridge or freezer until required. Place a layer of greased paper over the pastry. Place a dish of the same or similar shape and size on top of this. Cook in the oven for 4 minutes. Turn once during this cycle. Remove the top dish and paper, and cook the flan for a further 2 minutes. When pastry is cool, remove from flan dish and use as required.

Blackcurrant Flan
See illustration 7 in colour section

10 oz blackcurrants
4 oz caster sugar
1 baked flan in dish

Place blackcurrants and sugar in a covered dish. Cook for 3 minutes, stir and cook for a further 3 minutes uncovered. Cool the blackcurrants slightly, pour into the flan case and cook in the oven for a further 4 minutes. Serve hot or cold.

Cakes and Biscuits

It is surprising how often people arrive unexpectedly for tea or coffee when there is not a cake or biscuit in the house. That problem can be solved with the microwave oven, which enables cakes and biscuits to be produced in minutes. The oven is best suited for the cooking of light sponge cakes, not heavy fruit cakes. Care must be taken with the timing as cakes can easily be dried if left too long in the oven or cooking container.

HINTS FOR SUCCESSFUL CAKES

1   A variety of different-shaped cakes can be cooked in the oven as strong plastic, china and glass containers can be used. It is more convenient to use one container to bake in than two. The cake can be cut in half when cool.

Note: My favourite cake-cooking container is a round china soufflé dish which always gives perfect results.

2   Timings will vary according to the shape of the container used.

3   Always grease the container and line it with waxed paper or well-greased greaseproof paper at the base.

4   Do not cover the cakes during cooking, as they will tend to taste steamed.

5   Allow cake mix to stand for a few moments before placing in the oven.

6   Turn the dish during the cooking cycle for an even end result.

7   Test for doneness with a fine metal skewer as often the colour will not change during cooking.

8   Commercial cake mixes can be used in the oven; most are very acceptable.

DEFROSTING BY MICROWAVE

All types of cakes, bakery products and pastries can be defrosted in the oven. Care should be taken when items are filled with cream or butter icing. Place the frozen cake, etc., on to a piece of absorbent paper to defrost.

Food	Time
1 Danish pastry	30 secs
2 scones	1 min 15 secs
1 cream cake (8-inch)	1 min

Allow the food to stand for a few minutes before serving.

HEATING BY MICROWAVE

A doughnut or pastry, even a slice of cake, tastes fresher if it has been heated in the oven for just a few seconds before serving. This particularly applies to any product that has dried out since baking.

Walnut Tea Cake

2 oz butter
6 oz self-raising flour
2 oz soft brown sugar
1 egg
1 dessertspoon cornflour
¼ cup milk
For the topping:
2 tablespoons brown sugar
6 oz mixed chopped walnuts and glacé cherries
1 teaspoon mixed spice
2 dessertspoons jam
2 tablespoons self-raising flour
1 oz butter

Cream the sugar and butter for the cake well together. Add the egg and mix well. Stir in the flour, cornflour and milk. Pour half of the batter into a well-greased dish lined at the bottom. Mix all the ingredients for the topping together. Place half on top of the batter mix in the dish. Cover with the remaining cake batter. Top with the rest of the

71

topping. Even out and stand for 3 minutes before placing in the oven. Cook for 8 minutes or until firm to the touch. Allow to stand for 3 minutes before removing from baking dish. Loosen edges carefully with a palate knife. If a crisp topping is required, place cake under the grill for a few minutes.

Spicy Flapjack

3 oz margarine
4 oz golden syrup
2 oz soft brown sugar
2 oz currants
4 oz rolled oats
½ level teaspoon ginger

Grease well a round 8-inch Pyrex dish (do not use any type of plastic container for this recipe as it reaches a very high temperature). Place the fat, sugar and syrup together into the oven and heat for 3 minutes. Stir well. Add all the other ingredients and mix. Pour the mixture into the greased dish and even out. Cook in the oven for 5 minutes. Turn twice during this time. Leave to cool in the dish and mark out the cutting lines before it is firmly set. Store in an airtight container.

Marmalade Cake

6 oz soft brown sugar
6 oz margarine
3 eggs, separated
1½ oz ground almonds
8½ oz self-raising flour
3 level tablespoons chunky marmalade
2 oz chopped peel
grated rind and juice of orange
4 tablespoons water

Line the base of an 8-inch soufflé dish. Grease the sides and base well. Cook the peel by itself in the oven for 2 minutes. Cream together the sugar and margarine.

Gradually add the egg yolks, beating well. Stir in the peel, orange rind and juice, water and marmalade. Fold in the flour and almonds. Whisk the egg whites until stiff and gently fold into the cake mix. Turn into the baking dish and even out the top. Cook for 10 to 11 minutes in the oven, turning twice during the cooking cycle. Cool slightly and turn out of dish. The cake may be iced or left plain. Store in airtight container.

Tea-time Fingers

4 oz butter
2 large eggs
5 oz demerara sugar
6 oz self-raising flour
4 oz chocolate drops
4 oz sultanas
2 oz walnuts, chopped
½ teaspoon vanilla essence

Grease a dish approximately 11 in. × 7 in. Cream the butter and sugar together. Beat in the eggs until smooth. Mix in the flour, walnuts, sultanas, chocolate and vanilla essence. Pour the mix into a dish and even out. Allow to stand for 5 minutes before placing in the oven. Cook in the oven for 8 minutes or until firm. Turn twice during this cooking cycle. On removal of the dish from the oven, place under a hot grill until the surface is golden brown. Cut into fingers, allow to cool slightly and remove from dish. Store in an airtight container.

Scones

8 oz self-raising flour
1 oz butter or margarine
pinch of salt
1 oz caster sugar
milk

Rub the fat into the flour, add the salt and sugar, and mix with enough milk to make a soft dough. Roll out the dough about ½ inch thick and cut into rounds. Place six at a time in a circle in the oven on greaseproof paper. Cook for about 2½ minutes, turning once during this cycle. The scones can be placed under the grill for the surface to brown, if desired. If the scones should overcook in the oven, split them in half and serve them toasted with lots of butter. Cheese can be added instead of sugar.

Chocolate Gâteau
See illustration 8 in colour section

6 oz soft dark-brown sugar
8 oz butter
3 oz treacle
3 oz golden syrup
4 eggs
5 oz self-raising flour
1 oz coconut, dessicated
2 oz cocoa

Line the base of a round dish and grease well. Cream the butter, sugar with treacle and syrup together. Slowly add the beaten eggs plus a tablespoon of flour. Beat well. Fold in the sifted cocoa and flour. Add the coconut. Pour the mixture into the dish. Cook in the oven for 8 to 9 minutes. Turn once during this cycle. Turn cake out to cool. When cold, split and fill with cream. Decorate the top with cream and mandarin oranges.

Chocolate Biscuits

4 oz plain flour
1 level tablespoon cocoa
2½ oz butter
3 oz caster sugar

Rub the butter into the sifted flour and cocoa, add the sugar and mix well by hand until a soft dough is formed. Grease a sheet of paper and place in the oven. Press six small teaspoons of the mixture flat on to the paper, leaving space between each. Cook in the oven for 1½ minutes.

Turn once during this cycle. Remove from paper when slightly cooled. Leave plain or decorate with icing when cold. The mix will do about 12 biscuits.

Apple Cake

3 oz margarine
6 oz self-raising flour
3 oz soft brown sugar
1 teaspoon cinnamon
1 egg
5 tablespoons milk
2 cooking apples, peeled, cored and sliced
For the topping:
1½ oz flaked almonds
1½ oz soft brown sugar
½ teaspoon cinnamon
½ oz butter

Grease and line the base of a round, deep dish. Rub the margarine into the flour and add the cinnamon and sugar. Beat the egg and milk together and pour on to the flour slowly, mixing to a smooth batter. Add the apple slices, mix and place in the greased dish. Even out. Mix the ingredients for the topping together and sprinkle over the top of the cake. Cook in the oven for 6 to 7 minutes. Turn once during this cycle. The cake can be placed under the grill on removal from the oven to crisp the top. Allow to cool slightly before turning out from the dish.

Coconut Surprise

3 oz dessicated coconut
3 oz chopped glacé cherries
3 oz soft brown sugar
1 large egg

Grease well a shallow round dish. Beat together the sugar and the egg, and mix in the chopped cherries and the coconut. Pour into the greased dish and even out. Cook in the microwave oven for 5¼ minutes. Turn twice during this cycle. Remove the dish from the oven and allow to set. Mark the cutting lines. When cool, cut and place on cooling rack for 15 minutes before serving. This makes a firm, chewy biscuit.

Microwave Florentines

2 oz glacé cherries
3 oz walnuts
1 oz sultanas
1 oz blanched whole almonds
1 oz chopped mixed peel
1 oz plain flour
2 oz butter
2 oz demerara sugar
1 tablespoon syrup

Melt the butter, sugar and syrup together in the oven for 2 minutes. Chop the cherries, walnuts, almonds and sultanas. Add with the mixed peel and flour to the melted liquid. Mix well. Place four teaspoons of the mix on to greased paper in the oven. Place well apart. Cook for 2 minutes, turning once. Remove from the oven and shape edges neatly with the side of a fork. When slightly cooled, lift carefully on to cooling rack. When cool, the florentines can be coated with melted chocolate on one side. Makes 12 to 15.

Miscellaneous

This section contains bits and pieces – some short recipes for the oven and a note of some of its many other uses.

Pasta and Rice

Pasta and rice can be cooked in the microwave oven. Always add boiling water to the pasta and cook uncovered in a large container. Set the oven for the time recommended on the ingredients packet. Stir and give further time as required.

The microwave oven is the only appliance which can successfully reheat pasta and rice without drying it or losing the flavour. When heating pasta, cover the container, then fork gently before serving. To heat 8 oz of rice will take approximately 2 minutes; to heat 1 lb of macaroni cheese will take approximately 3½ minutes. Defrost frozen pasta and rice dishes in covered containers. Turn during the cycle and fork gently before heating.

Pastry

When defrosting, heating or cooking pastry in the microwave oven, the shorter the pastry the better the result. This is because steam is created in between the layers of flaky and puff pastry, making it wet. The filling inside a pie will tend to heat quicker than the pastry, as it usually contains a high fat or sugar content. The filling will transmit heat to the pastry — therefore when heating a pastry product do not leave it in the oven until the pastry feels hot as the centre will overheat. Heat pastry items on absorbent paper where possible. As the filling inside the pie, *e.g.* meat, can vary tremendously, times given below are only approximate guidelines.

Food	Time
Individual meat pie	1 min
Individual portion quiche	45 secs

Food	Time
One sausage roll	30 secs
Family-size meat pie	4–5 mins
Family-size flan	2½–3 mins

Raw frozen pastry items should be cooked in a conventional oven, but frozen precooked products can be defrosted and heated in the microwave. Rest product even when using a defrost control halfway through the cycle and before heating.

Food	Time
Family-size savoury flan	2 mins, rest 2 mins
Family-size fruit flan	2 mins; rest 1½ mins
Family-size meat pie	2½ mins; rest 2½ mins
Individual meat pie	45 secs; rest 45 secs

Scrambled Eggs

4 eggs
2 tablespoons milk
½ oz butter
salt and pepper

Beat together all of the ingredients in a glass container. Heat in the oven for 1 minute. Stir to break up the setting egg and return to the oven for 30 seconds. Stir and serve. If you require a drier egg, return the mix to the oven for a few seconds.

Poached Egg

Grease a small dish, break the egg into it, add a drop of melted butter, cover with a saucer and place in the oven. Cook for about 20 seconds. Allow to stand covered to finish cooking.

Porridge

1 cup porridge oats
1 cup milk
2 cups water
good pinch of salt

Mix all the ingredients together and place in the oven for 10 minutes. Stir twice during this cycle. For a quicker result use hot water or cook in individual bowls.

Hot Grapefruit

1 large grapefruit
2 teaspoons brown sugar
1 teaspoon ground ginger
1 teaspoon butter
2 teaspoons sherry

Cut the grapefruit in half, remove seeds and cut around segments. Place each half onto a serving dish. Sprinkle with the ground ginger and sugar, dot with butter and add the sherry. Place in the oven for 3½ minutes. This will keep hot for up to 10 minutes.

Stuffing for Chicken or Pork Dishes

1 small onion, finely chopped
2 oz peanuts, chopped
2 oz breadcrumbs
1 cooking apple, peeled, cored and sliced
1 dessertspoon chopped parsley
1½ oz butter
salt and pepper
lemon juice
½ teaspoon dried sage

Melt the butter in the oven for 45 seconds. Add the onion and peanuts and cook for 3 minutes. Add the sage, breadcrumbs, apple, parsley and 1 tablespoon of water. Stir and cover. Cook for 6 minutes. Season to taste with the salt, pepper and lemon juice. Use as required.

Chips and Roast Potatoes

After cutting potatoes into chips, place in the oven until warm and then fry in hot oil conventionally. This cuts down on frying time and gives a crisper chip. Blanch whole potatoes in the microwave for a few minutes before roasting.

Drying Herbs

Remove the leaves carefully from the stalks and place on a piece of absorbent paper. Put the herbs on paper into the oven and heat for 1 minute. Shake the paper gently and continue heating in 30-second periods until most of the leaves feel dry. Leave the leaves for 2 hours before placing into a jar. Flowers can be dried by the same method.

Other Handy Hints

Wine and beer bottles for home-made brewing can be washed and placed in the oven to kill yeast bacteria.

Butter from the refrigerator will be softened for spreading or baking by 20 seconds in the oven.

Dried apricots and prunes need not be soaked overnight. Pour boiling water over them and place in the oven for 1 minute (for approximately ½ lb). Leave them to stand for 5 minutes.

Don't scrape out jam jars – heat in the oven and see how much more you can get from them.

When cooking fruit cakes, heat the fruit and peel in the oven with a tablespoon of water before using.

To melt chocolate, place it in a bowl in the oven and heat for 1 minute. Stir and use.

To thaw out frozen orange juice in plastic containers, remove the top of the container and heat for 3 minutes on defrost.

For quick snacks on toast, prepare the toast and heat with cheese, baked beans or tomatoes for 1 minute in the oven.

Babies' bottles and teats can be washed and placed in the oven until hot. This will sterilise them safely.

PART THREE
Variable Power Control Microwave

The Variable Power Microwave Oven

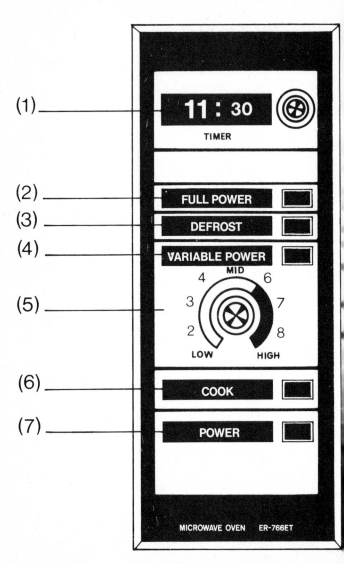

(1) — 11 : 30 TIMER

(2) — FULL POWER

(3) — DEFROST

(4) — VARIABLE POWER

(5) — MID 4 6 3 7 2 8 LOW HIGH

(6) — COOK

(7) — POWER

MICROWAVE OVEN ER-766ET

The Variable Power Control Microwave Oven works on the same principles as standard models, but it has greater flexibility of cooking control. You can alter not only the length of the cooking time but also the power level at which the food is cooked. This is similar to altering the temperature of a conventional oven. The oven has several additional controls, five buttons, a timer and a variable power selector. The oven is operated as follows:

1 Press the power switch in firmly to bring on the oven lights and cooling system.
2 Open the oven door and place the food inside. Close the door.
3 Select the power to be used, by pressing either Full Power (2), Defrost (3) or Variable Power (4).
4 If variable power is being used, turn the variable power dial (5) to the setting required.
5 Set the timer (1) for the required time.
6 Press the Cook button (6). At the end of the cooking time, a bell will ring. At any time during the cycle the oven can be stopped by opening the door and resetting as required.
7 To turn off the oven at the end of cooking, press the power switch (7).

Please do read the first two parts of this book before using the Variable Control Oven as they are applicable to it.

The following table is a summary of the foods you can cook with the variable power control settings:

Power level	Food items
High	Fish and vegetables
8	Hot drinks, sandwiches, suet
7	Reheating dishes and prepared meals
6	Chicken dishes, roasting meat
Middle	Defrosting over 4 lb, sauces
4	Eggs and cheese dishes
3	Defrosting 2–4 lb, stocks, soups, cakes
2	Casseroles, pies
Low	Defrosting under 2 lb, softening chocolate, butter and cheese

The recipes in the earlier sections of this book are ideal for using at the full power control of the oven, whereas those that follow are to show you how to use the power selector. Do remember that all the information given already on each food category is still relevant when using the selector.

SOUPS

When making a stock from bones, cook it at power 3 for 1½ hours. There will only need to be a 10 minute stand before using. When adding to a soup ingredients which are slow to cook – *e.g.* rice, barley, turnips, carrots – use power 3. Remember to stir every 15 minutes. Heat soups at high power.

FISH AND SEAFOOD

When cooking fish and seafood, use the high power and follow the cooking time and method in the Fish section earlier in the book. When heating fish dishes, use power level 6 for an even result without toughening.

BEEF

Power level 6 is good for cooking tender roasts, power level 3 for the slightly tougher joints. With casseroles, a higher power can be used for the more expensive cuts, lower power for the cheaper.

There is very little time saved when cooking some types of casserole in the microwave oven but the fuel saving is considerable and the end result good.

Beef with Mushrooms

1½ lb chuck steak, cubed
8 oz onions, sliced
garlic salt

1 tablespoon flour
2 tablespoons oil
small can condensed mushroom soup
4 oz mushrooms, sliced
2 oz black olives
7 fl oz water
1 teaspoon dried parsley
salt and pepper
small packet frozen peas

Heat the oil in the oven at high power for 1½ minutes. Toss the meat in the flour and heat in the oil for 5 minutes at high power. Stir well, add the onions and cook for a further 2 minutes. Stir in the parsley, pinch of garlic salt, salt and pepper, soup and water, and cook covered at power 4 for 30 minutes. Stir in the mushrooms and turn the oven down to power 2 for 30 minutes. Add the peas and olives, and cook for a further 35 minutes. Stir before serving.

Beef Casserole

2 lb stewing beef, cubed
1 tablespoon oil
1 dessertspoon Worcester sauce
2 onions, sliced
2 carrots, sliced
2 sticks celery
¾ pint beef stock
1 teaspoon made mustard
½ teaspoon mixed herbs
salt and pepper
flour

Heat the oil in the oven for 1 minute at high power. Add the vegetables and sauté at high power for 4 minutes. Dip the meat into the flour and add to the vegetables, stir and add all other ingredients. Cook covered at middle power for 15 minutes. Stir, turn down to power 2 and cook covered for 80 minutes. Stir every 20 minutes.

PORK, LAMB, VEAL

Cook joints at power 6, casseroles at a lower power.

Lamb Hotpot

1½ lb best end neck of lamb, chined
¾ lb potatoes, thinly sliced
2 onions, sliced
2 large carrots, sliced
salt and pepper
⅓ pint dry cider
pinch dried rosemary

Lay the lamb into a shallow dish, season and sprinkle with the rosemary. Cover with the onions and carrots, pour over the cider and lay the potatoes on top. Cover and cook in the oven at middle power for 20 minutes and turn down to power 2 for 50 minutes. Place under the grill before serving to colour potatoes.

Pork Casserole

½ oz margarine
1 onion, finely sliced
1 green pepper, finely sliced
1½ lb belly of pork, skinned and cubed
1 large carrot, finely sliced
2 tablespoons tomato purée
2 oz sultanas
½ pint chicken stock
salt and pepper

Brown the pork in a frying pan on the top of a conventional oven. Heat the margarine in the microwave oven for 1 minute at high power. Sauté the onion, carrot and pepper for 5 minutes at high power. Add the meat, stock and purée, stir well, cover and place in the oven at power 3 for 45 minutes. Add the sultanas and seasoning. Cook covered for a further 40 minutes. Stir every 20 minutes.

Barbecued Pork

4 pork chops
2 tablespoons oil
1 onion, finely chopped
4 tablespoons tomato purée
1 tablespoon lemon juice
2 tablespoons brown sugar
1 teaspoon mustard
salt and pepper
2 tablespoons vinegar
1 tablespoon water
1 teaspoon Worcester sauce

Heat the oil in the oven at high power for 1 minute. Sauté the onion for 1 minute. Add in all the ingredients except for the meat. Stir well. Heat at high power for 4 minutes. stir and leave to stand. Place the chops on a dish and cook at power 6 for 6 minutes. Turn over and cook for a further 6 minutes. Pour the sauce over the chops and heat for 7 minutes at power 6. Stir before serving.

POULTRY
Power 6 is ideal for cooking casseroles and whole birds.

Coq au Vin

3 lb chicken, jointed and skinned
1 oz butter
1 tablespoon oil
2 rashers bacon, cut into small pieces
1 large onion, sliced
½ pint red wine
salt and pepper
4 oz button mushrooms
1 bayleaf
mixed herbs

Heat the oil and butter in a frying pan. Fry the chicken joints until golden brown, place in a dish suitable for the microwave oven and add all the other ingredients. Cook covered at power 6 for 1 hour. Stir every 20 minutes.

VEGETABLES
High power is the most suitable for the cooking of vegetable dishes. Cooking times given in the Vegetables section earlier in the book can be followed.

EGGS
Egg dishes require slow cooking. Use power 4 for even consistency.

Crème Caramel

5 oz sugar
¼ pint water
1 pint milk
4 eggs

Place 4 oz of the sugar with the water into a heavy china or Pyrex dish. Place in the oven at high power for 3 minutes, stir and heat for 11 minutes (until starting to brown). Add 2 tablespoons hot water and stir with a wooden spoon. Heat the milk in the oven at high power for 3 minutes. Beat the eggs with the sugar and pour the milk over. Pour the egg mix over the caramel. Place the dish in a shallow water bath in the oven and cook at power 4 for 16 minutes, turning every 4 minutes. Leave to stand before serving.

CHEESE
To avoid toughening, cheese dishes can be cooked at power 4.

Cheese Shrimp Bake

8 slices white bread
1 large can of shrimps, drained and rinsed
2 sticks of celery, finely chopped

1 medium onion, finely chopped
1 small can condensed mushroom soup
dash of Worcester sauce
4 oz Cheddar cheese, grated
6 fl oz milk
3 eggs, beaten
2 oz butter

Place four slices of the bread in the base of a large shallow dish. Cover with the shrimp, onion and celery. Mix the soup with the sauce and pour over the shrimp mix. Sprinkle on the cheese and cover with the remaining bread. Beat together the eggs and the milk, pour over the bread and dot with the butter. Cover and set in the refrigerator for 30 minutes. Cook in the oven at power 4 for 30 minutes, turning twice during this time. Place under the grill if a crisp finish is required.

Use power 4 for the making of fondues.

Cheese and Bacon Flan

1 cooked flan case (leave in flan dish)
6 oz streaky bacon
1 small onion, finely chopped
5 oz grated cheese
2 eggs
½ pint milk
salt and pepper
½ teaspoon made mustard

Cook bacon on absorbent paper for 6 minutes at high power. Cut into small pieces and place on base of flan. Beat the eggs with the seasoning and mustard. Add the cheese, onion and milk. Stir and pour into the flan case. Place in the oven and cook at power 4 for 10 minutes, turn up to full power for 5 to 6 minutes until the surface is firm. Turn twice during this cycle. Garnish with tomatoes and leave to stand for 10 minutes before serving.

Macaroni Cheese

6 oz macaroni
1½ pints boiling water
1½ oz margarine
1½ oz flour
5 oz cheese grated
salt, pepper and pinch of mustard
1 pint milk
4 eggs

Place the macaroni in a deep dish and pour on to it the boiling water. Place in the oven uncovered and cook at full power for 15 minutes. Stir twice during the cooking period. Leave to stand for 5 minutes before draining. Heat the milk in the oven for 3 minutes at full power. Melt the butter at full power for 1¼ minutes. Stir in the flour and cook at medium power for 1¼ minutes. Add the milk slowly to the flour, mixing well. Add the seasoning and return to the oven. Heat for 2 minutes at mid power, stir and heat for a further 3 minutes. Stir in the grated cheese. Heat on power 4 for 5 minutes. Stir in the macaroni. Pour the mix into a large shallow dish. Make four wells in the mix and break one egg into each well. Cover and cook in the oven on power 4 for 6–8 minutes, until eggs are set. Sprinkle with crushed crisps before serving.

DESSERTS
Suet pastry is ideal cooked at power 8.

Baked Fruit Pudding

8 oz suet pastry
1 oz brown sugar
1 lb frozen blackberries
3 oz granulated sugar

Defrost the blackberries for 4 minutes on defrost. Grease a pie dish with butter and sprinkle with brown sugar. Line with the two-thirds of the suet pastry, fill with the blackberries and sugar, and cover with the remaining pastry. Cover with clear-wrap and cook in the oven for 8 minutes on setting 8.

Where eggs are being added to a dessert cook at low power.

Bread and Butter Pudding
8 slices bread and butter
4 oz raisins
2 oz sugar
2 eggs
1 pint milk

Grease a dish and place in it alternate layers of bread and butter with raisins and sugar. Beat the eggs with the milk, pour over the bread and leave to stand for 30 minutes in the refrigerator. Cook for 8 minutes at power 4. Leave to stand for 3 minutes before serving. For a crisp topping, place under the grill before serving.

Russian Pudding

1 lb apples, peeled, cored and cut into chunks
3 oz demerara sugar
1 oz butter
rind and juice of one lemon
1½ oz cornflour
1 pint milk
1 oz sugar
1 egg
nutmeg

Place in the oven the apples with the brown sugar, butter, rind and juice of the lemon. Cook for 3 minutes on power 8. Blend the cornflour with the milk, heat in the oven for 4 minutes on high power and stir after 2 minutes. Stir in the sugar and beaten egg, pour over the fruit and sprinkle with the grated nutmeg. Cook in the oven for 6 minutes on power 3.

CAKES

Cakes are best cooked on power 3, with the oven being turned up to a higher power for a perfect finish.

Gingerbread

4 oz margarine
3 oz brown sugar
2 eggs
¼ pint syrup
¼ pint treacle
½ teaspoon mixed spice
1 dessertspoon ginger
10 oz plain flour
pinch of salt
½ teaspoon bicarbonate of soda
¼ pint water

Melt the margarine, sugar, treacle and syrup together in the oven at high power for 3½ minutes. Sift the dry ingredients into the mix and add the water and beaten egg. Pour into a greased and lined shallow dish. Cook in the oven for 13 minutes at power 3, then turn up to power 6 for 7 minutes. Turn every 4 minutes.

Nut and Date Loaf

½ lb stoned and chopped dates
2 oz chopped walnuts
7 fl oz water
1 teaspoon bicarbonate of soda
6 oz soft brown sugar
1 oz butter
1 egg
8 oz plain flour
1 teaspoon baking powder

Heat the water in the oven on high power for 3 minutes, pour over the dates and stir in the bicarbonate of soda. Leave to stand for 10 minutes. Cream the sugar and butter together, add the egg and beat well. Fold in the flour and baking powder. Stir in the dates, liquid and nuts. Pour into a deep square dish which has been greased and lined. Cook in the oven at power 3 for 11 minutes and turn up to power 6 for 6 minutes. Turn three times while in the oven. Turn out and serve sliced with butter when cool.

BOTTLED FRUIT AND JAM

Bottled Plums

2 lb plums
1 lb caster sugar
½ pint water
1 × 4 lb kilner jar

Wash and stone plums. Put sugar and water in kilner jar; dissolve in microwave oven for 4 minutes on full power. Add plums and cover with cling-film. Microwave for 5 minutes at full power and for a further 5 minutes at mid power. On removal from oven, cover with lid of kilner jar and seal. Check that jar is sealed when cold.

Bottled Apples

2 lb apples
1 lb caster sugar
½ pint water
1 × 4 lb kilner jar

Wash and peel apples. Put sugar and water in kilner jar; dissolve in microwave oven for 4 minutes on full power. Add apples and cover with cling-film. Microwave for 2½ minutes at full power and for a further 2 minutes at mid power. On removal from the oven, cover with lid of kilner jar and seal. Check that jar is sealed when cold.

Blackcurrant Jam

1⅓ lb blackcurrants
1 lb caster sugar
¼ pint water
2 × 1 lb jam jars

Dissolve sugar and water in the microwave oven. Cook fruit for 4 minutes on full power. Mix ingredients together and microwave on full power for 3 minutes. Turn and microwave on full power for a further 3 minutes. Test for setting; if not set, microwave for a further 3 minutes. Divide into two jars.

Blackberry Jam

1⅓ lb blackberries
1 lb caster sugar
1 dessertspoon lemon juice
¼ pint water
2 × 1lb jam jars

Dissolve sugar and water in the microwave oven. Cook fruit for 4 minutes on full power. Mix ingredients together and microwave on full power for a further 4 minutes. Then microwave on mid power for 2 minutes. Test for setting; if not set, microwave for a further 3 minutes. Divide into two jars.

CHOCOLATE AND BUTTER
Chocolate should be melted at power 2. Butter can be softened at power 1.

HEATING WITH THE OVEN
When heating casseroles, pies, etc., for the family use a low power for a more even end result.
Note: Take care that the correct control buttons have been pressed. It is easy to press two buttons and forget the Cook button.

Index